LEADING
WITH
PURPOSE

LEADING WITH PURPOSE

The Transformative Power of Training on
Organizational Performance
(A Research Study with Biblical Perspective)

Dr. Sukoya T. Johnson, DSL

LEADING WITH PURPOSE

Published by Ten'e Publishing House
Duluth, Georgia

ISBN: 979-8-9994185-0-0

Printed in the United States of America

This book is dedicated to God —
For the vision, the strength, and the divine calling to lead with purpose.

To my husband and children —
Thank you for your unwavering love, patience, and the light you've shared with me throughout this journey.

To my parents —
To my mother, for your endless prayers and encouragement.
To my father, whose wisdom and strength continue to guide me from beyond.
Your love and example are the foundation on which I lead.

To my brother —
Thank you for always believing in me and pushing me forward with quiet strength and support.

To every person who has ever felt unseen in leadership —
This book is for you. May you lead boldly, train purposefully, and live fully in the calling

Contents

Chapter 1: Background of the Problem 11
Sets the stage for why leadership training matters, especially in underperforming government settings.

Chapter 2: Defining the Problem 15
Explores the core issues caused by inadequate training and the consequences on morale, retention, and performance.

Chapter 3: Purpose and Research Design 17
Outlines the study's purpose, goals, and research structure in accessible language.

Chapter 4: Methodology and Approach 21
Breaks down the research methods and rationale so readers can follow the process with ease.

Chapter 5: Conceptual and Theoretical Foundations 32
Covers key leadership theories like transformational, transactional, and path-goal leadership in real-world context.

List of Tables

<u>List of Figures</u>

Introduction

Training is imperative to the productivity of an organization. Organizational leaders that invest in effective training and development for their employees tend to achieve both short- and long-term benefits. The purpose of this flexible single case study was to explore the impact of training on organizational performance within a government organization. Path-goal theory, transactional leadership theory, and transformational leadership theory served as the conceptual framework for this study. Data collection involved in-person, structured interviews of 23 voluntary participants with the roles of manager, supervisor, and employee. Participant selection was based on convenience sampling due to work schedules and availability. The interview consisted of five demographic questions and nine interview questions. The researchers also took notes on participant behavior as well as ask follow-up questions which assisted in gauging accurate knowledge and experiences. Once interviews were completed, the researcher utilized the software NVivo to help with analysis through coding for common patterns and themes. Five themes emerged were (a) culture, (b) engagement, (c) resources, (d) training practices, and (e) leadership challenges. Findings show that participants were concerned with engagement, training, and resources. It may be beneficial to leaders to have reevaluated and tailor strategies to improve organizational performance for employees. In addition, these findings suggest that enhancing training strategies will provide a positive variation of motivational resources and opportunities. This approach will promote optimal performance which will retain employees and decrease barriers.

Key words: employees, leaders, leadership, training, organizational performance

Chapter 1

Background of the Problem

Section 1: Foundation of the Study

The impact of training is an important factor in determining the future of the organization. How a leader trains their employees on job specific duties can influence organizational efficiency (Iqbal et al., 2014). Training is necessary to enhance job performance and reflects the success of an organization. Employee evaluations conducted by leaders are important to assess knowledge and skills. If an employee requires more training, it is the responsibility of the leader to make sure those needs are met in a timely manner. The effects that training has on organizational performance are the focus of this research. The performance factors of an organization rely on the level or extent of training from a leader.

Employees are an imperative resource for an organization, and it is important to maximize their contribution to the organizational goals as a means of sustaining effective performance. This allows leaders to ensure that there is an adequate number of employees that are competent and capable of developmental growth in their specified career field. The question that may arise in many circumstances is why human resources are important. Keeping in mind that human resources are the intellectual part of the organization, employees should be a good source of gaining competitive advantage (Fernández-Esquinas, Pinto, Yruela, & Pereira, 2016), and effective training from leaders is the only way of developing organizational intelligence through building employee competencies in order to be successful. The authors state that leaders have to obtain and utilize human resources effectively. Therefore, organizations need to design its human resource management in a manner that fits into the organization's structure in order to achieve set goals and objectives. In addition, it is imperative that leaders assist their employees in obtaining the necessary skills needed, which increases performance, leads to commitment, retention, and decreases high employee turnover.

In order to manage an organization, it requires employees that are competent (Armstrong, 2009). According to the author, employees have the skills, knowledge, abilities, and competencies needed to work effectively which results in required training to acquire the necessary requisites to be able to make substantive contribution towards organizational performance. Training is imparting a specific skill to do a particular job while development deals with general enhancement and growth of individual skills and abilities through conscious and unconscious learning (Armstrong, 2009). The main purpose of effective training is to improve the employee competencies so that organizations can maximize efficiency and effectiveness of their human assets. Armstrong (2009) states that organizations could benefit from training and through winning the "heart and minds of" their employees in order to get them to identify with the organization, to exert themselves more on its behalf, and to remain with the organization. If employees experience flexibility and effectiveness on the job, they need to acquire and develop knowledge and skills, and if they are to believe that they are valued by the organization they work for, then they need to see visible signs of management's commitment to their training and career needs. Training is the process of investing in people so that they are equipped to perform well (Armstrong, 2009). This process is a part of an overall human resource management approach that hopefully will result in people being motivated to perform.

According to Cole (2002), training of employees remains an issue that has to be faced by every organization. However, the amount, quality, and quantity of training carried out by leaders vary tremendously from organization to organization. The author states that actors influencing the quantity and quality of training and activities are the degree of change in the internal and external environments. Many organizations meet their needs for training in an ad hoc and haphazard way (Cole, 2002). According to Cole (2002), training in these organizations is unplanned and unsystematic. However, other organizations identify their training needs, then design and implement training activities in a rational manner, and assess training results (Cole, 2002).

Chapter 2
Defining the Problem

The general problem to be addressed is lack of effective training from leaders to employees resulting in decreased organizational performance. Robinson (2016) argues that leaders are failing to train employees due to lack of prioritization in which tasks become overwhelming and training sessions take a back seat to process techniques which decreases performance. Jeelani, Albert, Azevedo, and Jaselskis (2017) indicate that leaders fail to effectively train employees because of passive instructional and lecture-based techniques that do not sufficiently engage workers. Research conducted by Legood, Schwarz, and Newman (2018) stated that 83% of surveyed employees were frustrated with failure to effectively train and procrastination from leaders because it negatively impacted organizational performance. This problem relates to leadership because failure to effectively train hinders organizational productivity. Poor leadership culture contributes to low retention rates; emotional well-being of subordinates and it plays a factor in subordinate engagement. Adequate training is imperative to maintain an efficient and effective organization. The specific problem to be addressed is the potential failure of leaders within a government organization, specifically Government organization to effectively train employees resulting in decreased organizational performance. A government organization can provide multiple services to residents and businesses. Sometimes when there is a variety of services that are being provided in one organization, effective training can be stagnant or overlooked. This is due to employees filling in where they are needed as opposed to being placed in a department where they are knowledgeable and honed skills.

Chapter 3

Purpose and Research Design

The purpose of this flexible single case study was to explore the impact of training on organizational performance within government organizations. The research found gaps between the present performance of an employee or group of employees, and the desired performance. It was explored through an in-depth study of employee training from leaders and whether it leads to a high turnover of employees. The lack of effective training poses a threat to productivity and the overall performance of an organization. The success of an organization relies upon the performance of employees. According to Kozlowski (2012), effective training practices boost performance and develop the skills, knowledge, and expertise of employees and the organization as a whole.

Research Questions

RQ1. How do leaders fail to effectively train employees within an organization?

RQ2. How do employees inhibit their own training?

RQ3. What types of training are effective and what types being ineffective?

These research questions explore how training programs affect the productivity of an organization. The questions identify the long-term effect of employee training in organizations. They focused on how the answers to these questions affect the overall performance of an organization in this competitive world. In addition, the answers enabled leaders to seek for means of promoting effective training. Management issues, overreliance on trial-and-error learning, assumptions of management that employees possess the necessary skills, time management, and lack of qualified trainers are the major attributes to ineffective training that should be dealt with (Wireman, 2010).

Research Question 1

Why do leaders fail to effectively train employees within an organization? This question seeks to clarify why leaders do not effectively train employees within an organization. Robinson (2016) suggests that leaders are only providing process techniques because they are not prioritizing overwhelming tasks. It relates to the problem statement because employee productivity within organizations is impacted based on the level of training received from organizational leaders. The failure of leaders to effectively train employees impacts employee development and performance.

Research Question 2

How do employees inhibit their own training? This question seeks to identify the ways that employees inhibit their own training when they are not being trained by leaders. According to Jeelani, Albert, Azevedo, and Jaselskis (2017), employee performance suffers when they have no knowledge or understanding of "why" they are performing specific tasks. This affects employee training because they are not obtaining viable information that leaders may have in order to make sure employees are well informed. When employees start training each other, they may spread misinformation to others and cut corners just to get the job done.

Research Question 3

What types of training are effective and what types are ineffective? Legood, Schwarz, and Newman (2018) argued that employee performance is negatively affected when not being effectively trained by leaders. This question seeks to identify what training is effective and ineffective for employees, which can affect employee performance. It is important for leaders to know and understand what types of training do and do not work for their employees. Leaders are responsible for making sure that employees have the knowledge and skills required to perform duties efficiently.

Chapter 4

Methodology and Approach

This section of the study is to gain an understanding of employee training from leaders with respect to organizational performance. The research design for this study is limited to using a flexible design, qualitative single case study methodology. Case study research is appropriate when there is a desire to interpret and understand the experiences of people in a bounded system. A system is bounded when there is a person, group, program, or situation that can be investigated in order to gain understanding of experiences or views of the members of the system (Lodico, Spaulding, & Voegtle, 2010). This study provides information on the researcher's positivism worldview and the methodology used to conduct research in an effort to seek answers to the research questions. Positivists are realists and believe that experience is important in determination rather than speculation (Brannick & Coghlan, 2016).

Discussion of Research Paradigms

A paradigm is the interpreted worldview of study from the researcher. It validates the researcher's opinion of the study and essentially how they view the world. There are four main research paradigms approaches that identify the researcher's worldview being studied: (a) Positivism (b) Post-Positivism (c) Constructivism and (d) Pragmatism. Positivism is based on experience of natural phenomena and relations (Pozzebon, 2017). Post-positivism is the acceptance of researcher influencing what is being observed by theories, background, knowledge, and values. The researcher stated that constructivism is the belief that knowledge is already gained in regard to the study based on prior experience. Moreover, pragmatism is based on the focus of practical approaches and solutions in situations.

This research used the positivist paradigm because it relies on hypothetical-deductive methods in order to verify priori hypotheses that are normally in quantitative methods, which is where functional relationships can be determined between independent variables and dependent variables (Su, 2018). In this case, the positivist researcher relied on qualitative methodology in examining the effects of training from leaders and the impact it has on organizational performance. Positivism places the focus on the idea of enhancing the strength of the relation between cause and effect in qualitative data and on trustworthiness and reliability (Brannick & Coghlan, 2016).

Discussion of Design

Deciding on a research design can be challenging. Using fixed designs are normally driven or it will be impossible to know in advance which variables need to be controlled and measured. Mixed methods designs can be fixed, and researchers need to be aware of the approach being used and consider which alternative is more appropriate. Fixed designs are used for pre-specification before reaching the main data collection stage (Robson, 2002). Fixed mixed method designs are mixed method studies where the use of quantitative and qualitative methods is planned at the beginning of the research process. Flexible designs evolve during data collection and are usually non-numerical (Robson, 2002).

This section of the study is to gain an understanding of employee training from leaders with respect to organizational performance. The research design for this study is limited to using a flexible design, qualitative single case study methodology. According to Lodico, Spaulding, and Voegtle (2010), case study research is appropriate when there is a desire to interpret and understand the experiences of people in a bounded system. A system is bounded when there is a person, group, program, or situation that can be investigated in order to gain understanding of experiences or views of the members of the system (Lodico, Spaulding, & Voegtle, 2010). This study provides information on the researcher's positivism worldview and the methodology used to conduct research in an effort to seek answers to the research questions. Positivists are realists and believe that experience is important in determination rather than speculation (Brannick & Coghlan, 2016).

Discussion of Method

Researchers that use qualitative, quantitative, or mixed methods should be privy to the underlying context, history, and political factors that affect the subject being studied. Mertens (2008), states that researchers use data collection methods that best work and serve their study. Methods are used to enable situations from cultural, economic, political, and historical perspective through focus group interviews, open-ended interviews, participant observation, journals, surveys, and questionnaires. There are five of the primary approaches to qualitative research methods. They are phenomenology, ground theory, ethnography, narrative, and case study (Creswell & Poth, 2018).

A method is a particular process for approaching something, especially a systematic or established one (Yin, 2009). Phenomenology is an objective method to conscious experiences in terms of actual existence and form without clouding it in terms of interpretations of causes and effects (Louchakova-Schwartz, 2018). Grounded theory is a research method that cancels out the standard procedures of research as its first step includes the collection of data and then extraction of main pointers for segmentation and analysis of a hypothesis and formation and testing of a theory (Konecki, 2018). Ethnography is qualitative research that aims is to scrutinize, understand and evaluate human lifestyle, societal formations and communal living (Holbraad et al., 2018). According to Webster and Mertowa (2007), narrative is a mode of inquiry in qualitative research, with a specified focus on the stories told by individuals. It explores what the story means and the lessons to be taught through a spoken or written text providing an account of an event or series of chronological events (Webster & Mertowa, 2007). Case study is a process or record of research in which detailed consideration is given to the development of a particular person, group, or situation over a period of time. It is a research strategy and an empirical inquiry that investigates a phenomenon within its real-life context (Yin, 2009). It is an intensive generalized study about an individual, a group or unit (Yin, 2009).

This study in particular, was conducted with a flexible design using qualitative methods specifically; a single case study design was used. Case study research is generally conducted through a systematic pattern following logic and accuracy. It is a research method where a phenomenon is investigated in its natural context and relies on in-depth research exploring underlying causes. Qualitative research helps to gain insights into the phenomena in question and is flexible in the sense that it helps in identifying the missing part of what is unknown or partially known (Creswell, 2014). According to Creswell (2014), qualitative research is more relevant in the context of discovery and is able to attain access to what was not known previously. The study focused on the single case study approach as a research strategy. The single case study approach is an in-depth study or investigation of a contemporary phenomenon using a source of evidence within its real-life context (Lodico, Spaulding, & Voegtle, 2010). According to Lodico, Spaulding, and Voegtle (2010), single case research is particularly useful when the phenomenon of interest is of a broad and complex nature and is best studied within the context in which it occurs. This study uses explanatory research, which focuses on the factors that affect the relationships between training and organizational performance.

Discussion of Triangulation

Triangulation is a type of method that is used to increase the validity of findings within the research. Validity draws trustworthiness of a study (Natow, 2020). It is concerned with the extent of accuracy from the concepts and data being evaluated. Triangulation ensures that single method biases are not a factor in the study. This method also explores complex human behavior by using various methods in order to offer an explanation that is more balanced (Natow, 2020). It provides confidence when using quantitative and qualitative studies. According to Natow (2020), there are four types of triangulations. The first type of triangulation is Data triangulation. It includes periods of time, space and people. The second type of triangulation is Investigator triangulation. It is the use of multiple researchers in a study. The third type of triangulation is Theory triangulation. It encourages different theoretical schemes in order to enable interpretation of a phenomenon. The fourth type of triangulation is Methodological triangulation. It promotes the use of data collection methods such as interviews and observations.

The type of triangulation that was used in this research is data triangulation. Data triangulation enhanced the analysis and interpretation of findings by interviewing several groups for verification. It attempts to map out and explain the richness and complexity of human behavior by studying it from more than one standpoint (Kennedy, 2009). In using this approach, the researcher can be more confident by increasing the credibility and validity of the findings when different methods yield the same results (Kennedy, 2009). According to the author, when a researcher uses only one group, they just have to believe that the findings are correct; however, when a researcher employs more than one group to answer a single question, 2 out of the 3 may produce same results or all 3 of them may produce clashing results. In addition, the researchers would either reframe the research question, reconsider the methods, or do both.

The author also noted that the researcher would ultimately arrive at a more complete and wholesome picture of the phenomenon. Data triangulation provides a more detailed and balanced picture of the situation (Altrichter et al. 1996). The need to interview different groups in order to obtain conclusive results in qualitative research can be justified from the fact that qualitative researchers are generally interested in investigating the "why" and "how" aspects and a single method cannot explain every aspect of every phenomenon (Altrichter et al. 1996). Qualitative methods are aimed at determining causality. In turn, a quantitative study is investigated on a statistical analysis of the data that is collected (Quinton & Reynolds, 2018). Data triangulation in training is a cross examination of raw data from multiple sources. In this study, the sources consist of managers, supervisors, and employees. The single questionnaire contained five demographic questions and seven interview process questions. In the first section of the questionnaire, the researcher collected demographic data to provide descriptive analysis for data triangulation purposes. This included the participant's age, gender, race, and how long they have worked for the organization. The second section of the questionnaire is the interview process which asks questions about the types of training being conducted. The interview questions helped the researcher collect information about how often the organization conducts training for the employees, whether the training increases productivity, performance, and skills, whether the training helps in task preparation, how employees conduct their own training; how much notice is given about the training date and time, and what materials are distributed. These questions assisted in understanding the approaches, methods, and techniques of training within the organization.

Summary of the Nature of the Study

This study was conducted with a flexible design using qualitative methods specifically; a single case study design was used. This research is to seek the reason for the lack of effective training from leaders to employees resulting in decreased organizational performance. Qualitative research is broad and can possess exploratory aims. The methodology is unique in approach depending on the ontological and epistemological stance, but stems from the motivation to explore, seek understanding, and establish the meaning of experiences from the perspective of those involved (Mertens, 2008). Through the use of triangulation, this study overcame biases and provided the researcher with confidence in the findings. From a positivist viewpoint, there is one single reality, which is independent of the individual and can be studied and measured through relativist or interpreter's perspective.

Chapter 5

Conceptual and Theoretical Foundations

The research framework focused on constructs, theories, actors, and constructs associated with training in organizations. This study uses the relationship between performance and process; seeks to clarify if training is a factor in organizational performance. Creswell (2014) suggests that the development of a well-informed research framework to guide a case study should improve consistency and trust. In qualitative case studies, having tangible resources of consistency in organizations allow for the research framework to support the case study findings that are imperative in order to meet objectives (Creswell, 2014). This qualitative single case study relies on theoretical basis through a conceptual framework. The conceptual framework assists in focusing attention on the data needed in order to contribute to theory.

Diagram

A diagram shows inputs and how the concepts, theories, actors, and constructs relate to each other. This conceptual framework provides a better understanding of the research problem.

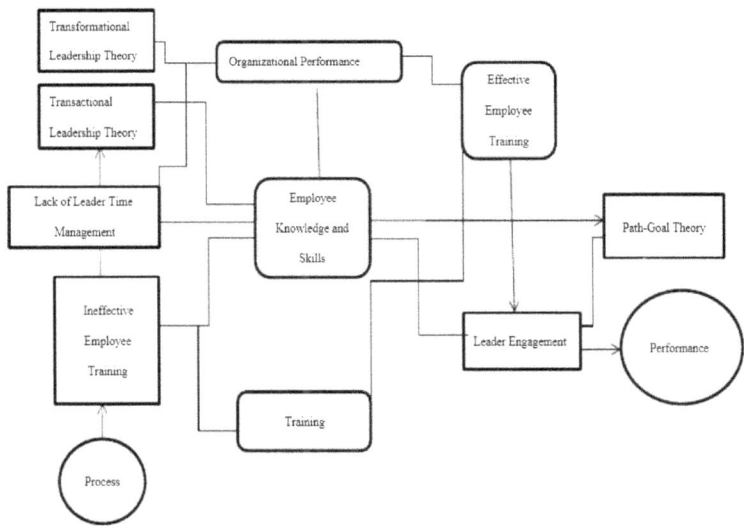

Figure 1. Relationships between concepts.
Note. The concept shows the constructs and how they relate to the performance or orientation process. Training is illustrated as affecting all constructs.

Concepts

A concept is a collection of meanings or characteristics associated with certain events, objects, conditions, situations, and behaviors (Brannick & Coghlan, 2016). According to Brannick and Coghlan (2016), it is the process of classifying and categorizing objects or events that have common characteristics beyond any single observation creates concepts. The researcher abstracts the meanings from experiences and uses words as labels to designate them then designs the hypotheses using concepts. The researcher then devises measurement concepts by which to test these hypothetical statements and collect data using the measurement concepts. The success of research hinges on how clearly it is conceptualized and how well others understand the concepts used (Brannick & Coghlan, 2016). The concepts that are discussed in this research are leader engagement and leader time management.

Leader Engagement. Leader engagement is the job of a leader to educate the organization, from top down, clearly identifying the path ahead (Mendes & Stander, 2011). This is done by engaging in the training of employees for clear direction and strategy. Organizational training supports strategic business objectives and meets the training needs that are common across projects and groups. Figure 1 shows how employee knowledge and skills are impacted through implementing path-goal theory and leader engagement. Leader engagement is connected to effective training for employees by building and strengthening relationships.

Leader Time Management. Time management is the process of planning and exercising conscious control of time spent on specific activities, especially to increase effectiveness, efficiency, and productivity (Claessens, van Eerde, Rutte & Roe, 2007). Productivity is increased when leaders manage their time by reducing workload and shortcuts. Figure 1 shows that leader's time management has an impact on employee training. When leaders do not manage their time for training, employees suffer in knowledge and skills (Claessens, van Eerde, Rutte & Roe, 2007).

Theories

Theories are principles that explain facts that have been repeatedly tested or are widely accepted and can be used to make predictions about natural phenomena (Abend, 2008). They are formulated to explain, predict, and understand phenomena and, in many cases, to challenge and extend existing knowledge within the limits of critical bounding assumptions (Abend, 2008). The structure of theoretical framework supports the research study theories. The theoretical framework introduces and describes the theory that explains why the research problem under study exists (Abend, 2008). The theories in this research are path-goal theory, transactional theory, and transformational theory.

Path-Goal Theory. Lunenburg (2011) suggested that there are roles that a leader must fulfill based on employee needs. This theory relates to the problem because it provides organizations with the understanding for needed effective training and to have the opportunity to strengthen leadership which provides skills and knowledge to employees in order to motivate and support them (Northouse, 2016). Figure 1 shows that path-goal theory encompasses the skills and knowledge of employees. It suggests that leaders have a responsibility to plan and set goals to manage their time in order to train employees to attain proficiency. Path-Goal theory places almost all of the responsibility on the shoulders of the leader. Moreover, there is a risk that employees become dependent on the leader and

fail to develop to the next level (Northouse, 2016).
Even though it is a complicated framework, it reminds
us that the purpose of leadership was to facilitate the
success of your subordinates.

Transactional Leadership Theory. Transactional
leadership theory has an impact on employee
motivation and performance. Transactional leaders
employ decreased engagement and employee self-
motivation, especially in training. They are concerned
with order, structure, and keeping up with the status
quo which can decrease employee performance
(Rodrigues & Ferreira, 2015). Figure 1 shows how
transactional leadership theory relates to employee
knowledge and skills which directly impact
organizational performance. Transactional leaders do
not manage their time adequately and can lead to
ineffective employee training. According to Rodrigues
and Ferreira (2015), transactional leaders do not pay a
lot of attention to organizational problems. Therefore,
there is a likelihood that employees will not receive the
training needed.

Transformational Leadership Theory.
Transformational leadership theory is focused on
employee motivation in which change is created, and

innovation shapes the organizational future (Peng, Liao, & Sun, 2020). A leader that is charismatic has the ability to connect with employees and motivate them toward achieving goals (Peng, Liao, & Sun, 2020). Transformational leaders foster a culture of employee independence and ownership that allows employees to grow. According to Peng, Liao, and Sun (2020), transformational leaders motivate followers to pursue higher goals in the interest of the organization by fostering connection and innovation.

Actors

Actors influence the development of research. They are key people that are vital to the research problem. The actors in this research are leaders, employees, and organizations.

Leaders. Leaders are managers and supervisors that ensure the work needed to be done is delivered. They make decisions, have the responsibility to delegate work related tasks to employees as needed, and ensure employees are trained adequately. The reason for this specific problem is that leaders are failing to effectively train employees. It is imperative to understand why this occurs within organizations.

According to Kirchner and Akdere (2017), they are held accountable for effectively training employees to the best of their abilities. The proper training of employees assists them in becoming future leaders (Kirchner & Akdere, 2017).

Employees. Employees being trained are resulting in increased or decreased performance standards (Kroll & Moynihan, 2015). Effective training from leaders is imperative to meet productivity standards and goals of the organization.

Organizations. The organizations in this research are government organizations. Government organizations are public sectors that offer a broad scope of training to employees from leaders.

Constructs

A construct is the building block of theories that assist in explaining how and why certain phenomena behave the way they do. It provides a common language and shared meaning that help us to communicate about things clearly and precisely. The constructs of this research are training, organizational performance, and employee knowledge and skills.

Training. Training is an independent construct. It can be effective or ineffective based on leader and employee engagement. It can pose a threat to productivity and the overall performance of an organization. Further, it affects employee turnover which results in orientation, motivation, and productivity which can limit the operation of the organization (Asfaw et al., 2015). Also, training can foster reform implementation which has an effect on information that is processed by employees. Training conveys basic information which prompts employees to implement those standards (Asfaw, Argaw, & Bayissa, 2015).

Organizational Performance. Organizational performance as a dependent construct seeks to identify variations of performance based on the lack of training from leaders to employees (March & Sutton, 1997). Training affects all aspects of performance from employees. The measurement of performance highlights the effectiveness of common practices within an organization.

Employee Knowledge and Skills. Employee knowledge and skills are imperative to organizational success. Berglund and Andersson (2012) suggest that leader investment in their employees by offering them effective training and opportunities for self-improvement boosts employee motivation and performance. The concept of knowledge refers to familiarity with factual information and theoretical concepts. Knowledge can be transferred from one person to another, or it can be self-acquired through observation and study. However, skills refer to the ability to apply knowledge to specific situations. Skills are developed through practice, through a combination of sensory input and output.

Relationship Between Concepts, Theories, Actors, and Constructs

Training can be effective or ineffective based on leader and employee engagement. It can pose a threat to productivity and the overall performance of an organization. Further, it affects employee turnover which results in orientation, motivation, and productivity which can limit the operation of the organization (Asfaw, Argaw, & Bayissa, 2015). Organizational performance is the foundation of the concept. Through organizational performance, the researcher seeks to identify variations in performance based on the lack of training from leaders to employees

(March & Sutton, 1997). Figure 1 shows that employee knowledge and skills are imperative to organizational performance. Berglund and Andersson (2012) suggest that leader engagement in their employees by offering them effective training and opportunities for self-improvement boosts employee motivation and performance.

Summary of the Research Framework

The research framework is based on path-goal theory, transactional leadership theory, and transformational leadership theory with the concepts of leader engagement and leader time management. Leader time management includes providing employees with the appropriate knowledge and skills needed through training in order to produce optimal performance within an organization (Claessens, van Eerde, Rutte & Roe, 2007). Figure 1 shows the relationship between the four elements associated with the research framework. With organizational performance as a foundation of the study, the researcher indicates that each element presented affects one another. It is the overall factor in whether employees are being effectively trained by their leaders.

Definition of Terms

Organizational analysis: Organizational analysis refers to employee resources that are present in an effort to assist in competencies that can be managed when leaders are managing their employees' competencies (Susomrith, Coetzer, & Ampofo, 2019). It suggests that leader management should be consistent with basic organizational requirements such as efficiency and quality.

Operational analysis: Operational analysis refers to the tasks needed to be performed at the desired knowledge, skill, and attitude level (Susomrith, Coetzer, & Ampofo, 2019). According to the researcher, the methods for performing task analysis are through questionnaires, interviews, observations, and reports.

Individual analysis: Individual analysis refers to examining the cause of events in individual leaders or employees. It allows the measurement of expectations and learning requirements of employees (Susomrith, Coetzer, & Ampofo, 2019).

Assumptions, Limitations, Delimitations

Assumptions, limitations, and delimitations are imperative to the research process (Ellis & Levy, 2009). These categories are the fundamental basis of the study regardless of the type of research that is being performed (Ellis & Levy, 2009). They explain and frame applicable contents of the study. Ellis and Levy (2009) argued that a study is incomplete if the assumptions, limitations, and delimitations are not discussed. The assumptions of this study describe the facts that are presumed to be true but not verified. Limitations are the weaknesses that can hinder study. Delimitations refer to how the boundaries or conditions ultimately impacted the study.

Assumptions

Assumptions are defined as what the researcher believes is true but has yet to be proven (Ellis & Levy, 2009). The study of specific phenomenon that does not have factual evidence are deemed assumptions (Cameron, 2012). Assumptions are vital research components and are necessary in comprising the study

(Ellis & Levy, 2009). There are four assumptions that exist within the context of this study. The first assumption is that there are specific reasons, outside of the scope of this study, why some leaders succeed and why others fail at effectively training their employees. Aarons, Ehrhart, Moullin, Torres, & Green (2017) found that one program had succeeded in changing leader attitudes about how to manage, but a follow-up study revealed that other leaders had then regressed to their pre-training views. Researchers stated that the only exceptions were those whose leaders practiced and believed in the new leadership style the training was designed to teach. The second assumption is that effective training from leaders to employees has a positive effect on organizational performance. Organizations that develop good training in accordance to the need of employees as well as to the organization always receive positive results (Lindebaum & Zundel, 2013).

The third assumption is that, through anonymous surveys, participants provide truthful answers. The fourth assumption is that each participant provided accurate responses describing the phenomena of their work-related experiences. To provide a safe environment for participants to express their true opinions specific parameters were taken to ensure that anonymity and confidentiality are preserved for each participant (Leedy & Ormrod, 2019).

Limitations

Limitations are weaknesses within a study (Ellis & Levy, 2009). This study focuses on a government organization. Therefore, the results of this study cannot be generalized because the limitations for training from leaders to employees include data in other locations. Even though this study can reveal efficacious leadership practices of an organization in a specific location, the results can vary in other government organizations. To support this single case study, this is a limitation that can only be lifted if the research was performed on various government organizations and/or location. Another limitation to this study is that there is only one researcher responsible for collecting, analyzing, and interpreting the data using the appropriate methods for reducing or limiting personal bias. This can be accomplished through the use of random sampling. In random sampling, the researcher provided each individual in a broad target population an equal opportunity to participate. The assistant manager for the organization provided a list of employees that were available. The researcher randomly provided participants with a number ranging from 1 through 23. In addition, it is important to be transparent and honest in the research approach.

Delimitations

Delimitations refer to the scope of the study (Ellis & Levy, 2009). It determines what can be controlled within the boundaries of the study. As it relates to this study, it is inclusive of a single government organization within the United States of America. Permission was granted by the manager of the organization. The interviewees were managers, supervisors, as well as employees.

Chapter 6

Relevance and Real-World Impact

The significance of the study highlights how the research was beneficial to the development of science and the society as a whole. The researcher signifies a broader sense of the problem and gradually narrows it down in order to demonstrate the specific group that benefited from the study. This is done by applying the relevant research questions, assumptions, limitations, and delimitations that are applicable to the research.

The purpose of this qualitative, single case study was to explore the impact of training on organizational performance within the government. Through data collected from leaders, and employees from a specified government organization, the researcher provided recommendations that can help improve organizational performance. The success of an organization relies on leaders who are competent and possess the ability to maintain proficient performance from their employees. It is the responsibility of leaders to positively influence their employees to perform at levels that meet or exceed organizational standards. Leadership development is essential to expanding the knowledge and ability of leaders in order to increase organizational performance. According to Low and Ang (2012), effective leadership has the tenancy to increase organizational profits. Ineffective training from leaders hinders their ability to effectively motivate employees (Lindebaum & Zundel, 2013). Exploration of effective training, employee performance, and organizational sustainment for the government can provide a greater understanding of situations and strategies for improvements. As a result of leaders implementing effective training strategies, government organizations can achieve profitability and successful outcomes (Ulrich, Zenger, & Smallwood, 2013).

Reduction of Gaps in Literature

Through the years, gaps in effective training have been greatly reduced (Kodwani & Prashar, 2019). It is believed that a leader orchestrating a needs assessment is imperative for effective training. A needs assessment assists in identifying gaps between the leader's ideal level of performance and the current level of performance for employees. In addition, it prioritizes relevant resources in an effort to reduce those gaps. According to the researchers, training needs should be defined as gaps between knowledge, skills, and attitudes that the job demands and currently possessed by the trainee. Training needs is an ongoing process to collect information to identify gaps that can be developed to assist in meeting organizational objectives. Assessing training needs is one of the most important areas of developing training programs. It can diagnose current training problems and predict challenges in the future. The process of identifying training needs depends on the gap between the existing performance ability and desired performance. Employee evaluations and performance appraisal are also helpful. Susomrith, Coetzer, and Ampofo (2019) found that organizational training needs are determined at the request of top-level management, but for the most part has been identified by first-line supervisors. Some of the gaps in effective training are organizational, operational, and individual analysis.

Organizational analysis suggests that leader management should be consistent with basic organizational requirements such as efficiency and quality (Susomrith, Coetzer, & Ampofo, 2019). This study contributed to the reduction of gaps in effective training from leaders to employees by identifying competency deficiencies, training approaches, and leader prioritization. Issues in employee competencies stem from a lack of engaged development. According to Santhanam, Dyaram, and Ziegler (2017), being able to identify gaps in competency is the first step toward correcting ineffective training. Analyzing how employees currently perform and what areas that they are lacking can assist leaders in their training approach. How leaders approach their employees with training is equally important. Training should be conducted at a time and place that benefits both the leader and employee. In addition, training should not be attempted when tensions are high between both individuals and at the spur of the moment. Leaders prioritizing employee training session's benefits time management and how efficient the task processes are taught for each individual. Some employees may require additional training in order to understand and perform certain tasks. This is something that leaders need to take into consideration. Failure to analyze training needs can hinder benefits and become a financial burden for the organization.

Implications for Biblical Integration

Biblical principles are fundamental truths; however, laws may be for specific circumstances (Deuteronomy 22:8, KJV). Biblical principles are important in effective training because they hold leaders, employees, and the organization to an ethical standard. Some of these challenges are straightforward and to the point; however, others are complex and require reflection. In addition, biblical principles in effective training provide a comprehensive insight on problems that hinder organizational performance (Melé & Fontrodona, 2017). Moreover, biblical principles assist in exploring resources for moral guidance and ethical consideration. Ethical approaches in research specifically in regard to training and the impact that it has on organizational performance, helps in the understanding of the complex nature of ethical decision making (Sparks & Pan, 2010). James 3.13-15 reads "Who is wise and understanding among you? Let him show it by his good life, by deeds done in the humility that comes from wisdom. But if you harbor bitter envy and selfish ambition in your hearts, do not boast about it or deny the truth. Such "wisdom" does not come down from heaven but is earthly, unspiritual, of the devil. For where you have envy and selfish ambition, there you find disorder and every evil practice" (The Holy Bible, 2020).

Providing biblical principles in this research can help evaluate ethical systems in an organization while in engaging normal operational activities. The use of performing a flexible design case study through qualitative methodology can analyze and provide review and discussion of the applicable questions that provided a guide for the participants (Melé & Fontrodona, 2017). It provided faith and trust from the participants to the researcher and into the research itself. Those who are followers of Christ appreciate the real-world realities of the research as a resource for guidance.

The research of training in organizations were conducted from the positivism philosophy which adheres to the view of factual knowledge that is gained through observation and analysis of qualitative methodology which can prove trustworthiness (Mendes & Stander, 2011). In positivist studies, the role of the researcher is limited to data collection and interpretation in an objective way. Positivism is dependent on observations that are reliable in accordance with the empiricist view that knowledge stems from human experience. Moreover, in positivist studies, the researcher is independent from the study and there are no provisions for human interests within the study. Mendes and Stander (2011) argue that as a general rule, positivist studies usually adopt deductive approach, whereas inductive research approach is usually associated with a phenomenology philosophy.

When it comes to leaders effectively training their employees, stepping up and showing strength in the ability to perform the task given by Jesus, to the best of their ability, should be the top priority on the list. Providing employees with the knowledge and skills that they need is imperative to not only the organization, but also human development. According to The Holy Bible (2020), Jesus took upon him the form of a servant to his disciples (Philippians 2:7, NIV). It showed humility and how the place of a leader is to serve their followers. This is in relation to applying principles to their needs in an effort to make them perform their job better. When leaders do not meet these needs, they fail at the basic task that was bestowed upon them.

Benefit and Relationship to the Leadership Practice

According to Higgs and Rowland (2005), it is important that leadership practices improve in organizations because employee performance could hinder business longevity. Business failures prompt leaders to reduce costs, increase revenues, improve productivity, reduce cycle time, infuse technology, and improve product quality. Longenecker (2010) states that ineffective leadership practices make performance improvement difficult or nonexistent. Effective communication from leaders to employees is imperative in order to train adequately. The problems that leaders have relating to communication are not listening, lack of sharing information, and ineffective interpersonal relationships (Longenecker, 2010). Ineffective communication practices damage a leader's performance. In addition to communication, leaders fail to effectively manage their time with priorities and create a situation where they are too busy to train adequately (Longenecker, 2010). This is due to organizational change and an increase in productivity levels which prompt leaders to become stressed or burned out. When leaders are stressed or burned out, it may enable them to demonstrate the inability to handle pressure in certain situations, communicate, make sound decisions, or adequately train employees (Longenecker, 2010). In return, the confidence of their employees may be hindered as a result.

Summary of the Significance of the Study

This qualitative, single case study explores the impact of training on organizational performance within the government. The collected interview data from this government organization provided recommendations to improve organizational performance. It is the responsibility of leaders to ensure that their employees are competent and proficient in their performance. It is imperative that leaders effectively train their employees in order to develop the employees into future leaders within the organization. According to Low and Ang (2012), this improves employee retainability and has the tenancy to increase profit. Leaders that do not train effectively risk a lack of employee motivation, which can hinder recommendations for improvement and successful outcomes (Lindebaum & Zundel, 2013).

Chapter 7

Review of Professional and Academic Literature

This literature review includes the effects of training on organizational performance. The literature sub-sections focus on the following: leadership practices, engagement, time management, path-goal theory, transactional theory, transformational theory, and training. Literature review provides an in-depth discussion of the research topic with the intention of providing a better understanding of relevant information through related studies.

Leadership Practices

According to Higgs and Rowland (2005), it is important that leadership practices improve in organizations because employee performance could hinder business longevity. Business failures prompt leaders to reduce costs, increase revenues, improve productivity, reduce cycle time, infuse technology, and improve product quality.

Longenecker (2010) states that ineffective leadership practices make performance improvement difficult or nonexistent. Effective communication from leaders to employees is imperative in order to train adequately. The problems that leaders have relating to communication are not listening, lack of sharing information, and ineffective interpersonal relationships. Ineffective communication practices damage a leader's performance. In addition to communication, leaders fail to effectively manage their time with priorities and create a situation where they are too busy to train adequately. This is due to organizational change and an increase in productivity levels which prompt leaders to become stressed or burned out. When leaders are stressed or burned out, it may enable them to demonstrate the inability to handle pressure in certain situations, communicate, make sound decisions, or adequately train employees. In return, the confidence of their employees may be hindered as a result.

Yukl (2010) states that improving leadership practices are concerned, strong leadership theories and research exist in literature that examine leader engagement, leader time management, path-goal theory, transactional leadership theory and transformational leadership theory. However, there is very little research and discussion on the subject of leadership practices, effectiveness and training in the context of rapidly changing organizations (Cockerell, 2009). This context is imperative because as the demands brought on by competition and the need for organizational transformation evoke a large amount of pressure on leaders within an organization to attain new competencies or improve competencies that already exist and compete in the changing business environment (Murray and Richardson, 2003). The question comes to mind of "What type of specific skill or competency issues confronts effective training from leaders?" The answer to this question has important career success and performance implications for leaders and the organizations where they are responsible for effectively training employees.

Longenecker (2010) notes that previous research shows that there are deficiencies in leadership practices that can result in significant performance and career advancement problems for employees. This problem is exacerbated and becomes even more challenging when leaders are called to lead and perform in changing and dynamic environments. This is true for several reasons. First, leaders that are operating in these types of environments, where their current skill sets are being put to the test, must develop new skills in the heat of battle. Secondly, to make this task even more challenging, managers are frequently performing in environments where they receive little feedback on their performance. Even though this lack of feedback is not uncommon, it is exacerbated immensely in times of change (Longnecker, 2010). Leaders can easily find themselves with issues that they might not be aware of which can damage their ability to deliver better training to the employees in their organization at a time when high performance is imperative. In addition, this can hinder the performance and development of an entire organization.

Longenecker (2010) states that there is substantial research that makes it clear that feedback is critically important during training in order to help leaders properly align their actions while making adjustments to improve their leadership practices. While feedback is important to improve organizational performance, multisource feedback devices, when properly implemented, have been found to be an invaluable source of performance information for leaders dealing with training (Conger & Toegel, 2003). The author found that multisource feedback has proven to be one of the most important innovations in leadership practices over the past 20 years. In this study, the multisource processes were utilized to better understand the training issues that leaders can ly experience in periods of organizational change. Moreover, it can be viewed as a vital piece of individual analysis within a needs assessment which is the foundation of effective training.

The Problem

According to Fernández-Esquinas, Pinto, Yruela, and Pereira (2016), organizations are experiencing an increase in competition due to globalization, changes in technology, politics, and the economy. This situation prompts leaders to train employees in order to prepare them for adjustment to the environmental changes which enhance performance.

Zhang, MacKenzie, Jones-Evans, and Huggins (2016) mention that there is substantial evidence citing the growth of career knowledge and skills in the business sector within the last two decades. This growth has not only been brought about by improvements in technology and a combination of factors of production, but also by increased efforts towards development of leadership. It is in every organization's responsibility to enhance the performance of employees and implement effective training practices. Employees are an imperative resource for an organization, and it is important to maximize their contribution to the organizational goals as a means of sustaining effective performance. This allows leaders to ensure that there is an adequate number of employees that are competent and capable of developmental growth in their specified career field. The question that may arise in many circumstances is why human resources are important.

Fernández-Esquinas, Pinto, Yruela, and Pereira (2016) found that human resources are the intellectual part of the organization, employees should be a good source of gaining competitive advantage, and effective training from leaders is the only way of developing organizational intelligence through building employee competencies in order to be successful. Leaders have to obtain and utilize human resources effectively. Therefore, organizations need to design its human resource management in a manner that fits into the organization's structure in order to achieve set goals and objectives. In addition, it is imperative that leaders assist their employees in obtaining the necessary skills needed, which increases performance, leads to commitment, retention, and decreases high employee turnover.

Concepts

According to Brannick and Coghlan (2016), a concept is a collection of meanings or characteristics associated with certain events, objects, conditions, situations, and behaviors. It is the process of classifying and categorizing objects or events that have common characteristics beyond any single observation that creates concepts. The researcher abstracts the meanings from experiences and uses words as labels to designate them then designs the hypotheses using concepts. The author then devises measurement concepts by which to test these hypothetical statements and collect data using the measurement concepts. The success of research hinges on how clearly it is conceptualized and how well others understand the concepts used. The concepts that are discussed in this research are leader engagement and leader time management.

Leader Engagement

Mendes and Stander (2011) interpret leader engagement to be the job of a leader to educate the organization, from top down, clearly identifying the path ahead. This is done by engaging in the training of employees for clear direction and strategy. Organizational training supports strategic business objectives and meets the training needs that are common across projects and groups. Figure 1 shows how employee knowledge and skills is impacted through implementing path-goal theory and leader engagement. Leader engagement is connected to effective training for employees by building and strengthening relationships.

Mendes and Stander (2011) state that focusing on engagement is imperative because leaders have to understand who in the organization is developmentally ready and who may need more training in order to move forward. During times like this, a certain pattern of behavior sets into many organizations. Generally, leaders creating strategy are living in the future, concentrated on trends. They are imagining the next quarter's time frame. Meanwhile, employees generally function in the present and are concentrating on accomplishing daily tasks. Many employees find it difficult to shift into the mindset of future strategy and need time to process. According to the researchers, it is the responsibility of a leader to educate their employees from the top, down while identifying the training path ahead. The challenge is to continue to move forward, with employees feeling more than just clear and confident about the strategy and direction, but also excited and invigorated. As a leader in today's business environment, the leader is the human energy of a business. Leaders build a sense of engagement, helping employees realize their growth for the organization, the team, and themselves. Engagement is the combination of the perception of changes and events happening around the leader and the level of energy that is experienced. Leaders that are engaged with employees have a positive perception of changes around them and they produce high quality work. Lack of trust, inconsistent leadership, and fear of job stability were some reasons for disengagement (Mendes & Stander, 2011). It is acknowledged that leader engagement is important to organization.

Heldenbrand and Simms (2012) researched training that could help improve leader engagement when training was developed with engagement as a focus. The research was an 8-month study that included 45 participants at a long-term nursing facility that were interviewed. The participants were interviewed with the understanding of what improved leader engagement. The researchers stated that training was more effective to improve leader engagement when skills from the training were built into employee daily responsibilities. A constraint of their training practices was that those involved in the training did not work for the leaders that actually had the decision-making authority. Heldenbrand and Simms (2012) reported that this may have slowed down the process for implementing skills that are learned and was the main cause of negative training practice feedback. The study resulted in new leadership approaches in order to enhance decision-making and increase the participation of leaders, as well as to improve efforts to engage with more employees.

According to Gallup (2015), the impact of leader engagement is important to an organization. Leader engagement is linked to several important organizational outcomes. It was reported that 30% of leaders were not actively engaged in the organization. The study was comprised of 400,000 employees who found that leaders who were not engaged were not adequately trained themselves or were too overwhelmed with other tasks. In return, employees were not performing up to standards, and disengaged in their career choice (Gallup, 2015). It was also stated that leaders were responsible for at least 70% of employee engagement variance scores in. If leaders lacked adequate training, employees chose to leave their jobs due to negative development. Employees that had leaders that were engaged were 59% more likely to also be engaged than those that had disengaged leaders (Gallup, 2015).

Cho and Lewis (2011) performed a study that included 2,551 leaders. Of the leaders, 54% were flanked with high engagement and motivation ratings. They were also noted to be assertive, accountable, and strong decision makers. Organizations that possess high leader engagement were found to have contributed to higher organizational profits and lower employee absenteeism and turnover. Engagement is connected to all aspects of organizational outcomes, including employee turnover and productivity (Cho & Lewis, 2011).

According to Marrelli (2001), a study that was analyzed by the 2007 U.S. Merit Promotion Board Report found that organizations that lacked engagement had three areas of training that were lower than organizations that had high engagement. The responses were analyzed utilizing the five-point Likert scale that included choices from strongly agrees to strongly disagree. The two positive responses and two negative responses were combined in order to make three responses. There were three statements for employees to choose from: (a) my training needs were assessed by my leader (38%/51%); (b) I am satisfied with training in my present job (46%/58%); and (c) I am given an opportunity to improve my skills (47%/63%) (Marrelli, 2001). The percentages that were lower derived from organizations that lacked engagement, and the higher percentages came from high leader engagement organizations.

Leader Time Management

Claessens, van Eerde, Rutte, and Roe (2007) define leader time management as the process of planning and exercising conscious control of time spent on specific activities, especially to increase effectiveness, efficiency, and productivity. Productivity is increased when leaders manage their time by reducing workload and ineffective shortcuts. Figure 1 shows that leader's time management has an impact on employee training. When leaders do not manage their time for training, employees suffer in knowledge and skills.

According to Peeters and Rutte (2005), leaders feel that they do not have enough time. Working under the assumption that longer hours lead to improved productivity, they drive themselves and others to increase efficiency. Leaders are expected to be highly productive; however, there is a sense of individual and collective slippage, less than optimal work performance, and impending burnout. The ability of leaders to manage the increase in both workload and burnout effectively is vital because their behavior has a significant impact on others. The authors state that under stress, leaders are more defensive and make poor decisions. This is especially costly for leaders because they set the tone for their organizations. Their moods affect how employees think and behave, in which they also tend to mimic their leader (Peeters & Rutte, 2005).

Green and Skinner (2005) suggest that time management is a behavior aimed at achieving an effective use of time while performing goal-directed activities. This highlights that the use of time is not an aim in itself and cannot be pursued in isolation. The focus is on goal-directed activity, such as performing an organizational task which is carried out in a way that implies that the use of time is effective. These behaviors are:

o   Time assessment behaviors, which aim at the awareness of here and now, past, present, future, and self-awareness of one's time use, which help to accept tasks and responsibilities that fit within the limit of an individual's capabilities (Wratcher and Jones, 1988).

o   Planning behaviors, such as setting goals, planning tasks, prioritizing, making to-do lists, and grouping tasks which aim at an effective use of time (Macan, 1996).

o   Monitoring behaviors, which aim at observing one's use of time while performing activities, generating a feedback loop that allows a limit to the influence of interruptions by others (Zijlstra et al., 1999).

Leader Time Management and Transactional Leadership

According to Sarfraz (2017), transactional leaders focus on routine responsibilities, activities, and efficiency.   Strategic leaders focus on continuous learning. Their time management skills require concentration and focus, prioritization, and time management. Concentration, prioritization, and focus are needed to determine task importance and completion methods for these leaders. Time management complements transactional leaders because it provides them with ease in making complex decisions.

Leader Time Management and Transformational Leadership

According to Sarfraz (2017), when it comes to transformational leaders, they are focused on time management skills that allow them to transmit their visions to employees. Transformational leaders achieve through inspiring employees to create changes in themselves that they can rely on in the future. They tend to set goals in order to ensure that the smaller goals and tasks build a pathway toward a bigger vision.

Theories

According to Abend (2008), theories are principles that explain facts that have been repeatedly tested or are widely accepted and can be used to make predictions about natural phenomena. They are formulated to explain, predict, and understand phenomena and, in many cases, to challenge and extend existing knowledge within the limits of critical bounding assumptions. The structure of theoretical framework supports the research study theories. The theoretical framework introduces and describes the theory that explains why the research problem under study exists. The theories in this research are path-goal theory, transactional theory, and transformational theory.

Path-Goal Theory

Lunenburg (2011) suggests that there are roles that a leader must fulfill based on employee needs. Northouse (2016) relates this theory to the problem because it provides organizations with the understanding for needed effective training and to have the opportunity to strengthen leadership which provides skills and knowledge to employees in order to motivate and support them. Figure 1 shows that path-goal theory encompasses the skills and knowledge of employees. It suggests that leaders have a responsibility to plan and set goals to manage their time in order to train employees to attain proficiency. Path-Goal theory places almost all of the responsibility on the shoulders of the leader. Moreover, there is a risk that employees become dependent on the leader and fail to develop to the next level. Even though it is a complicated framework, it reminds us that the purpose of leadership was to facilitate the success of your subordinates.

According to Farhan (2018), leaders have to be effective in their roles in order to provide support, guidance, and advice to employees. Training programs have to be designed and curated in their optimal form to result in maximum success. House (1971) states that path-goal theory states that a leader's behavior is contingent to the satisfaction, motivation and performance of their employees. The job of a leader is viewed as guiding employees to choose the best path in order to reach both their goals as well as the goal of the organizations. This theory argues that leaders have to engage in different types of leadership behavior that is dependent upon the nature and the demands of the situation. It is the leader's job to help employees attain goals and provide them with direction and support that is needed in order to ensure organizational goals are met (Farhan, 2018). Path–goal theory allows leaders to be flexible and adjust their leadership style as needed.

According to House (1971), path-goal theory encapsulates the necessity for specific role a leader has to fulfill, as well as the leadership traits leaders should acquire in their practice. In addition, House (1971) provided guidelines of leaders must follow in order to compensate for employee skill issues.

Leadership Theories

According to Bickle (2017), the first theory is the trait theory of leadership; it is believed that leaders share certain inborn personality traits, such as drive, ambition, and self-confidence. The second learning theory is a behavioral one, where researchers studied the behavioral aspects of effective leaders, such as their ability to motivate people and their communication skills. The third, contingency theory, advocated that it is the environmental factors surrounding leaders that influenced their ascent to leadership, and that it is not so much their leadership qualities as it is about the situation in which they needed to lead. According to the researcher, the fourth and final theory is the transformational leadership theory, which suggests that good leaders are those able to stimulate, transform, and use the values, beliefs, and needs of their employees in order to accomplish tasks.

Overcoming Challenges and Obstacles with the Path Goal Theory

Bickle (2017) states that challenges and obstacles are inevitable in the organization, which is why a strategy should be implemented to avoid and evade these. Providing employees with the necessary tools to resolve issues ensures organizational success in training is not hindered.

Goal Achievement

According to Bickle (2017), effective leadership not only guides employees in the right direction towards their goals but also requires leaders to assist in the identification of goals and objectives from the start. Goals should be achievable, realistic, and measurable.

Boosted Employee Productivity and Motivation

Effective leaders understand the importance of rewarding and recognizing employees through the offer of incentives and intrinsic motivation (Bickle, 2017). This drives employees to succeed and reach their maximum for the benefit of the entire organization. According to Bickle (2017), gamification is a widely employed strategy by organizations in order to significantly boost the engagement and information absorption of learners. It encapsulates the implementation of gaming elements into serious course content, such as star bars, point scores, leader boards and real prizing.

Enhanced Support Network

Bickle (2017) states that having a supportive leadership style ensures that interactions remain learner-centered, meaning that employees' personal preferences and emotional needs are accounted for, and are at the center of decision-making. When employees feel respected and valued, they are more likely to develop a stronger bond with the organization and tend to work harder.

Increase Employee Confidence with Path Goal Theory

When employees' confidence levels increase, barriers built around their learning are broken down, resulting in them wanting to learn more (Bickle, 2017). Path-goal theory allows for this through the participative leadership approach, were confident, employees can control their own personal training path. Increased confidence can be achieved by leaders' constant acknowledgment of employees, praising them for their good work, and providing frequent feedback (Bickle, 2017).

Functional and Positive Environment

According to Bickle (2017), a functional and positive environment is nurtured when the path-goal theory is used when leaders are effectively training employees as communication and collaboration are involved daily within an organization which evokes a happy and peaceful work area. Having a work area that is happy and peaceful alleviates stress which results in employees wanting to be more productive and performing effectively (Bickle, 2017).

Transactional Leadership Theory

Rodrigues and Ferreira (2015) state that transactional leadership theory has an impact on employee motivation and performance. Transactional leaders employ decreased engagement and employee self-motivation, especially in training. They are concerned with order, structure, and keeping up with the status quo which can decrease employee performance. Figure 1 shows how transactional leadership theory relates to employee knowledge and skills which directly impact organizational performance. According to Rodrigues and Ferreira (2015), transactional leaders do not manage their time adequately and can lead to ineffective employee training. In addition, the authors state that transactional leaders do not pay a lot of attention to organizational problems. Therefore, there is a likelihood that employees have not received training needed (Rodrigues & Ferreira, 2015).

Breevaart et al. (2014) state that transactional leadership theory rewards and punishments are contingent upon employee performance. The leader views the relationship between managers and employees as a give and take exchange. When employees perform well, they will be rewarded. When employees perform poorly, they are punished in some way. Rules, procedures, and standards are imperative in transactional leadership. This type of leadership monitors employees carefully in order to enforce rules, reward success, and punish failure. However, it is not a catalyst for growth and change within an organization. Instead, transactional leadership theory is focused on maintaining the status quo and enforcing current rules and expectations. This type of leader tends to be good at setting expectations and standards that maximize organizational efficiency and productivity. They generally provide constructive feedback regarding employee performance and allow group members to improve their performance in order to obtain better feedback and reinforcement from leaders. Transactional leadership does not encourage creativity in order to seek new solutions to problems (Breevaart et al., 2014). Research has found that this theory is more effective in situations where problems are simplified and clear.

According to Kuhnert and Lewis (2017), transactional leadership can work well in crisis situations where the focus needs to be on accomplishing certain tasks. By assigning clearly defined tasks to employees, leaders can ensure that they are getting accomplished. While transactional leadership can be useful in some situations, it is considered insufficient in many cases and may prevent both leaders and followers from achieving their full.

Transformational Leadership Theory

Peng, Liao, and Sun (2020) explain that transformational leadership theory is focused on employee motivation in which change is created, and innovation shapes the organizational future. A leader that is charismatic has the ability to connect with employees and motivate them toward achieving goals. Transformational leaders foster a culture of employee independence and ownership that allows employees to grow. The authors suggest that transformational leaders motivate followers to pursue higher goals in the interest of the organization by fostering connection and innovation.

Transformational Theory and Organizational Performance

According to Antonakis, Avolio, and Sivasubramaniam (2003), transformational leadership is an imperative to organizational performance. It is one of the ways to enhance an individual or group performance. Leaders that are transformational can motivate their employees to explore current and new prospects. Transformational leadership theory helps the employees attain goals that have high standards. Transformational leaders move beyond immediate self-interest. It creates an environment where employees are motivated. Motivated employees that work in a supportive climate provide more effective customer service, reinforce organizational performance, and contribute to financial gains for shareholders.

Gumusluoğlu and Ilsev (2009) suggest four dimensions of transformational leadership style which includes idealized influence, inspirational motivation, intellectual simulation and individualized consideration. The behaviors that are accepted in this theory are motivation, intellectual challenge, inspiration, and individual consideration. They are considered as a core function of outstanding leaders that could be familiar around the world. Leaders are more attentive toward the needs of their employees, which is imperative for their growth and achievements. Gumusluoğlu and Ilsev (2009) argued that transformational leaders provide positive feedback to their employees, which motivate them to show more effort, and encourage them to be innovative toward complex issues. Therefore, employees tend to behave in a way that simplifies high levels of task performance. In addition, transformational leaders encourage employees to weigh more for collective profit of organizations and leaders over personal interests.

Jung et al. (2003) conducted research on transformational leadership to understand the connection between transformational leadership and performance. It was found that transformational leaders affect employee performance through the development of a strong bond with employees. This theory increases the emotional connection or identification between the leader and employee in a way that employee is more confident to perform beyond expectations. Leaders have a positive effect on the effect of employee performance. The researcher suggests that transformational leadership is linked to innovative capabilities and is defined as a leadership style that transforms employees to rise above their self-interest by altering their morale, ideals, interests and values. This motivates the employees to perform better than initially expected. It motivates employees to achieve past expectations and encourages them to look past their own self-interest for the betterment of an organization. The researcher also provided indirect support for the statements and suggested that those leaders who demand conceptual values and engage in knowledgeable incentive that give meaning to their organization and employee work.

Constructs & Variables

According to Caputi, Viney, Walker, and Crittenden (2011), constructs are the building blocks of theories that assist in explaining how and why certain phenomena behave the way they do. They provide a common language and shared meaning that help to communicate about things clearly and precisely. The constructs of this research are training, organizational performance, and employee knowledge and skills.

Training

Asfaw, Argaw, and Bayissa (2015) note that training is an independent construct. It can be effective or ineffective based on leader and employee engagement. It can pose a threat to productivity and the overall performance of an organization. Furthermore, it affects employee turnover which results in orientation, motivation, and productivity which can limit the operation of the organization. Also, training can foster reform implementation which influences information that is processed by employees. Training conveys basic information which prompts employees to implement those standards.

Beardwell, Holden and Claydon (2004) state that training has been long recognized and attracted a lot of research attention from academic writers. This has yielded into a variety of definitions of training. The researchers define training as the planned and systematic modification of behavior through learning events, activities, and programs that result in the participants achieving the levels of knowledge, skills, competencies, and abilities needed to effectively for their job. As researchers continue with their quest into the training research area, they also continue their arguments into its importance. Some of these researchers argue that the recognition of the importance of training in recent years has been heavily influenced by sector competition and the relative success of organizations where investment in employee development is highly emphasized (Beardwell et al., 2004). The researchers add that technological developments and organizational change have gradually led some leaders to the realization that success relies on the skills and abilities of their employees, which is why there is a need for effective and continuous investment in training and development.

Benefits of Training

Cole (2017) explains that the main purpose of training is to acquire and improve knowledge, skills and attitudes towards job related tasks. It is one of the most vital motivators which can lead to both short-term and long-term benefits for leaders, employees, and organizations. There are many benefits associated with training. The researcher summarizes that these benefits as follows:

- o High morale – employees who receive training have increased confidence and motivations.

- o Lower cost of production – training eliminates risks because trained personnel are able to make better and economic use of material and equipment thereby reducing and avoiding waste.
- o Lower turnover – training brings a sense of security at the workplace which in turn reduces labor turnover and absenteeism is avoided.
- o Change management – training helps to manage change by increasing the understanding and involvement of employees in the change process and also provides the skills and abilities needed to adjust to new situations.
- o Provides recognition, enhanced responsibility and the possibility of increased pay and promotion.
- o Help improve the availability and quality of staff.

Human Resource Training Needs

According to Wognum (2001), training and needs may occur at three organizational levels. These levels are (1) strategic level where needs are determined by top management while considering organizations goals, mission, strategy and problems, which need to be resolved or fixed; (2) tactical level where needs are determined with middle management while considering developments needs to the coordination and cooperation between organization units, and (3) operational level where needs are determined with lower executive management and other employees while considering problems related to operations such as performance problems of individual workers and departments in subject. An organization has to formulate human resource training goals which will enable both formal practices in order to create a workforce that is effective and competitive (Wognum, 2001). This provides proper coordination as well as proper incorporation of the needs within the three levels. The first issue is to identify the needs relevant to the organization's objectives.

Torrington et al. (2005) state that there are three categories of identifying training and development needs. These categories are: (1) resolving problems: this focuses on employee performance; (2) improving current work practices: this focuses on improvement regardless of the performance problems; and (3) changing or renewing the organization situation, which may arise because of innovations or changes in strategy. In addition, many approaches have been made to identifying needs. These are the problem-centered (performance gap) and profile comparison (changes and skills) approaches. Similarly, several approaches for analyzing training needs depending on whether they are new or current employees in prior studies have been discussed (Torrington et al., 2005). The two most common approaches being the problem centered approach and the profile comparison approach. The problem-centered approach focuses on any performance difficulties and the organizational analyses if the problems are due to insufficient skills, which then need to be developed if the problem is going to be solved. On the other hand, a profile comparison approach focuses on matching the competencies with the job that is filled, whether it is a new or current position. Some changes in strategy and technology may also require the need for new or additional skills (Torrington et al., 2005).

Effect of Training on Performance

Purcell, Kinnie, and Hutchinson (2003) find that organizational growth and development is affected by several factors. In light with the present research during the development of organizations, employee training is imperative to improve performance as well as increasing productivity. In turn, this leads to placing organizations in the better positions to face competition and stay at the top of their sector. Therefore, this implies that there is a significant difference between the organizations that effectively train their employees and organizations that do not.

Wright and Geroy (2001) note that employee competencies change through effective training practices. This not only improves the overall performance of the employees to effectively perform their job, but it also enhances their knowledge and attitude which contributes to superior organizational performance. Prior research on training and organizational performance discovered findings regarding its relationship to one another. Training has generated performance improvement related benefits for the employee as well as for the organization by positively influencing employee performance through the development of employee knowledge, skills, ability, competencies and behavior.

Swart et al. (2005) elaborate on training as a means of dealing with skills issues and performance gaps as a way of improving employee performance. Bridging the performance gap refers to implementing a relevant training intervention for the sake of developing particular skills and abilities of the employees and enhancing employee performance. The researchers explain the concept by stating that training facilitates an organization to recognize that its employees are not performing well and their knowledge, skills, and attitudes have to be molded according to the organization's needs. This is necessary in order for the employees to possess a certain amount of knowledge related to different jobs. However, training is not enough. Employees have to constantly adapt to new requirements of job performance. In other words, organizations need to have continuous policies of training and retaining of employees and not to wait for occurrences of skill and performance gaps.

According to Wright and Geroy (2001), effective employee training from leaders enables competencies that implement job related work efficiently and achieve objectives in a competitive manner. Moreover, complaints of dissatisfaction, absenteeism, and turnover can be reduced when employees are effectively trained and can experience satisfaction associated with the sense of achievement and knowledge that they are developing their inherent capabilities. Most benefits that result from training are easily attained when training is planned. This means that the organization, leaders, and employees are prepared for the training in advance. Planned training is the deliberate intervention aimed at achieving the learning necessary for improved organizational performance (Wright & Geroy, 2001). Planned training consists of the following steps:

- o Identify and define training needs
- o Define the learning required in terms of what skills and knowledge have to be acquired
- o Change attitudes toward learning
- o Define the objectives of the training
- o Plan training practices to meet the needs and objectives by using the right combination for training techniques and locations
- o Decide who provides the training
- o Evaluation training
- o Amend and extend the training as necessary

Organizational Performance

March and Sutton (1997) find organizational performance as a dependent construct seeking to identify variations in performance based on the lack of training from leaders to employees. Training affects all aspects of performance from employees.

Armstrong (2000) states that organizational performance is generally associated in terms of outcomes. However, it can also be associated with behavior. Organizational performance is measured against the performance standards set by an organization. There are many measures that can be taken into consideration when measuring performance. These measures are using productivity, efficiency, effectiveness, quality, and profitability.

Wood and Stangster (2002) express that profitability is the ability to earn profits consistently over a period of time. It is the ratio of gross profit to sales or return on capital employed. Efficiency is the ability to produce the desired outcomes by using as minimal resources as possible, while effectiveness is the ability of employees to meet the desired objectives or targets. Productivity is expressed as a ratio of output to that of input. It is a measure of how the individual, organization, and industry convert input resources into goods and services. The measure of how much output is produced per unit of resources employed. Quality is the characteristic of products or services that bear an ability to satisfy the stated or implied needs. It is to consistently achieve better products and services at a progressively more competitive price.

According to Paauwe (2004), organizational performance is conceptualized as a multidimensional construct with studies measuring it in different ways. It is the ultimate dependent variable that researchers can use to justify investment in training and includes human resource, operational, and financial performance dimensions (Tharenou et al., 2007). However, some studies use the term organizational effectiveness, conceptualized as a broader and more general construct that focuses on internal organizational performance in comparison to organizational performance measures that are mainly focused on accounting and financial outcomes.

Tharenou et al. (2007), suggest that scholars operate organizational performance using objective and subjective measures or both. Most studies utilize subjective measures including, in some cases, a composite index or a single organizational performance item. Organizational performance includes three categories which are human resources, organizational, and financial related. Human resources have proximal outcomes such as collective KSAs, motivation, employee turnover, job satisfaction, and organizational commitment (Dyer & Reeves, 1995). Operational outcomes are distal outcomes that are comprised by labor productivity, innovation, customer service, and customer retention (Rauch & Hatak, 2016). Financial outcomes are comprised of three categories as: (a) financial performance, (b) product market performance, and (c) shareholder return (Richard et al.,

2009). The financial performance category comprises measures of profit, return on assets, and return on investment. Product market performance comprises measures such as sales and market share, and shareholder return includes measures such as total shareholder returns and economic value added.

As noted by Draft (1988), it is the responsibility of leadership to ensure that their organizations strive to achieve high performance levels. Therefore, leaders have to set the desired levels of performance for any periods in question. This setting goals and standards can be accomplished by setting goals and standards against which an employee's performance can be measured. Organizations ensure that their employees are contributing to producing high quality products and services through organizational performance management. This management process encourages employees to get involved in planning for the organization and participates by having a role in the entire process which creates motivation for high performance levels. Managing organization performance includes activities that ensure that organizational goals are being consistently met in an effective and efficient manner. It can focus on the performance of the employees, a department, processes to build a product or service.

According to Kinicki and Kreitner (2007), the productivity of employees has shown that employees who are effectively trained by their leaders are satisfied with their job will have higher job performance, and job retention, than those who are not happy with their jobs. In addition, organizational performance is higher in happy and satisfied employees and leaders find it easier to motivate high performers in order to attain firm targets.

Possible Ineffective Organizational Leadership

According to Einarsen et al. (2007), negative personal attributes of a leader can contribute to ineffectiveness. At the lowest level, leaders that are ineffective can be known as being passive. This type of leadership is called laissez-faire. Laissez-faire leadership is a very passive approach towards leading and does not show interest in their responsibilities (Einarsen et al., 2007). It is in violation of organizational interests when poor efficiency is visible and possibly undermines the motivation, well-being, and job satisfaction of employees. Furthermore, researchers argue that leaders may become obsessed by power and personal authority which may resort to narcissism, self-serving, and self-centered behaviors, wrongful use of power, manipulation, intimidation, coercion and one-way communication. This type of leadership can derail training efforts as well as trust from employees (Padilla et al., 2007). However, ineffective leadership may also be due to negative personal attributes of leaders. Researchers call these negative attributes because they impede effective leadership and the resulting leadership is sometimes can be toxic, or destructive.

The consequences of laissez-faire leadership, negative leadership, toxic leadership or destructive leadership can affect employees, organizations, stakeholders, and even leaders themselves (Kellerman, 2004). Therefore, employees may suffer from poor psychological health, lack of interest, low job performance, poor organizational citizenship and low self-confidence, organizations may suffer from high turnover rates and low productivity, and leaders may suffer from lack of personal influence, derailment, demotion, and personal psychological suffrage (Harvey et al., 2007).

Judge et al. (2002) also showed that individuals with negative traits had less chance of emerging as leaders. Even if they were able to reach leadership positions, they were rated as fewer effective leaders. Zaccaro et al. (2004) also noted that destructive personal attributes contribute to harmful and negative leadership influences. However, the researcher noted that destructive organizational outcomes are not necessarily caused by destructive leaders. Padilla et al. (2007) suggest that toxic leaders that have negative organizational outcomes are also due to susceptible employees and conducive environments. Susceptible employees conform to their passive leaders that have power because their unmet needs make them vulnerable to these influences. Lastly, favorable factors that underpin destructive leadership are instability, perceived threat, cultural values, and absence of checks and balances, and institutionalization. Toxic leadership is based on the interaction of the leader's characteristics and the situation. This interaction can promote discretionary actions on the part of the leader that harms the well-being of organizational members and long-term organizational performance (Padilla et al.,2007). Therefore, in order to overcome discretionary actions, organizations must take appropriate actions to create a working environment that encourages positive behaviors in organizational members.

Employee Knowledge and Skills

Berglund and Andersson (2012) suggest that leader investment in their employees by offering them effective training and opportunities for self-improvement boosts employee motivation and performance. Employee knowledge and skills are imperative to organizational success.

Hughes, Zajac, Woods, and Salas (2020) state that effective training requires assessment of needs, planning, instructional design, and appropriate tools as well as a repository of training process data. The main components of training include an effectively managed training process, documented plans, personnel with appropriate mastery of specific disciplines and other areas of knowledge, and mechanisms for measuring the effectiveness of the training program. Identifying training needs is generally based on the skills that are required to perform the organization's set of standard processes. Specific skills may be efficiently and effectively imparted through other forms of practice rather than in-class training. Other skills require more formalized training sessions, such as in a classroom, provided through web-based training, through guided self-study, or from a formalized on-the-job training program. The researchers say that formal or informal training sessions employed for each situation should be based on an assessment of the need for training and the performance gap to be addressed. Success in training can be measured in terms of the availability of opportunities to acquire the knowledge and skills needed in order to perform new and ongoing organizational objectives. Knowledge and skills can be technical, organizational, or contextual. Technical skills pertain to the ability to use the equipment, tools, materials, data, and processes required by a project or a process. Organizational skills pertain to behavior within and according to the employee's organization structure, role and responsibilities, and general operating principles and methods. Contextual skills are the self-management, communication, and interpersonal abilities needed to successfully perform in the organizational and social context of the project and support groups (Hughes, Zajac, Woods, & Salas, 2020).

Related Studies

According to NG (2017), training practices from leaders to employees in a commercial industry do have an impact on organizational performance. In related studies, there is research that suggests training is ineffective when it is predictable. Effective training from leaders to employees helps to increase retention and enhance employee knowledge and skills. Employees tend to be less enthusiastic about training when the training becomes predictable. An uninteresting approach to training can cause employees to be disengaged and unmotivated in learning about their job. This causes training to be ineffective and hinders organizational strategies. The researcher suggests that if training is necessary, it should be done in the form of the Six Sigma game in order to engage and motivate employees.

Petkova (2011) researched the optimization of training effectiveness which addressed the need to integrate research on a regulatory fit between theory and training effectiveness. Findings revealed that a series of favorable training outcomes were observed when training programs fit the learners' basic motivational orientation from leaders.

Nagar (2009) studied the effectiveness of training practices being conducted by the commercial banks in both public as well as in the private sector. The findings revealed that training programs are generally effective with respect to the selected variables of the study, which include trainer, teaching, and computer-aided program and infrastructure facilities.

Al-Ajlouni, Athamneh, and Jaradat (2010) stressed that when evaluating training practice, there is a need to compare the output with other similar training programs. This comparison would be of help in identifying problems and weaknesses, which could be the basis of the trainer in his or her future training program.

According to Eidt (1992), everyone learns at a different pace and have different ways of learning. This study suggests that training impedes time management; therefore, employees should naturally learn as they go. Learning tasks as you go maximizes valuable time and production activities. This brings pride to employees and promotes self-efficacy. The researcher believes that teamwork versus individual contribution is a problem and ineffective training is counterproductive.

Table 1. Related Studies

Author	Topic	Title	Source	Findings
Al-Ajlouni, Athamneh, and Jaradat (2010)	A comprehensive literature review of training evaluation practices and comparison of training programs	Methods of evaluation: Training techniques international research	Journal of Finance and Economics, 37, 56-65.	Leaders should identify problems and weaknesses, which could be the basis of the trainer in his or her future training program
Eidt (1992)	A literature review of the effectiveness of training practices conducted by commercial banks in public and private sectors	Applying Quality to R&D Means 'Learn-As-You-Go'	Research Technology Management, 35(4), 24.	Training impedes time management; therefore, employees should naturally learn as they go
Nagar (2009)		Measuring training effectiveness	The Indian Journal of Commerce, 62(4), 86-90.	
NG (2017)	A comprehensive literature review of ineffective predictable training			Training programs are generally effective with the trainer, teaching, and

Petkova (2011)	A comprehensive literature review of ineffective predictable training	A complete project environment simulation to improve six sigma training class engagement	International Journal of Quality Innovation, 3(1), 1-15.	computer-aided program and infrastructure facilities
	A review of the optimization of training effectiveness addressing the need to integrate regulatory fit between theory and training effectiveness.	Optimizing training effectiveness: The role of regulatory fit.	The University of Akron, OH.	Author suggests that should be done in the form of the Six Sigma game to engage and motivate employees
				A series of favorable training outcomes were observed when training programs fit the learners' basic motivational orientation from leaders.

Anticipated Themes and Discovered Themes

According to EL Hajjar and Alkhanaizi (2018), themes are derived from data and prior theoretical understanding of the phenomenon being studied. The training techniques range from computers to labor intensive processes that provide known advantages and disadvantages. The themes presented are training contents, training environments, facilities and materials, training schedule, and presentation style. Training contents are an important part of effective training.

Ramachandran (2010) conducted an analytical study on the training effectiveness of public sector employees. The outcome of the study showed that there was a difference in employee perception on the basis of demographic characteristics and training effectiveness. In addition, it was also found that experiences and education are predominating and determining factors of training practices.

Sanjeevkumar and Yanan (2011) found that factors affecting employee training when combining theoretical and empirical research. The problem addressed in their study also included factors that affect training: training contents, training environment, training schedule, presentation style, and employees' personal characteristics training of effectiveness.

McNamara (2016) stated that selection of training activities improves the teaching and learning process, which include sessions led by instructors, computer-based training, and web-based training, and self-directed, interactive, or multimedia-inspired lessons. Providing various platforms allows employees to maximize their knowledge, skills, and attitude toward the training being received from leaders. Training environments are important because they enable a positive environment for learning.

Orey (2014) found that the key to an effective training environment is a leader that has a positive attitude and a good training facility. Training facilities such as auditoriums offer a flexible and technologically advanced learning environment. Another factor that may affect training effectiveness is training materials that leaders utilize. The purpose of utilizing training material was to promote employee involvement, encouragement, and comprehension. It increases employee learning experience. Another factor that affects training effectiveness is the training schedule.

Silverman (2015) explained that a training schedule allows for time to address relevant problems that may occur and assists in finding effective solutions to any related contingencies, which may arise during the training process. Another theme that affects effective training is how leaders present training to their employees. Leaders motivate employees and increase their desire to learn and remember new ideas and skills through their training presentation style.

Factors Affecting Training Effectiveness

Training content is an important factor in training effectiveness. McNamara (2016) found that it is important to select training activities that will improve the teaching and learning process, which include instructor-led sessions, computer-based training, web-based training, and self-directed, interactive, or multimedia-inspired lessons. By selecting the most suitable media and materials, trainees may be able to maximize their skills, knowledge, and attitude toward the training program. During the development phase, training design has to be piloted in order to ensure the content is understandable and applicable for employees to learn. There are many important points should be taken into account such as the accuracy of the contents, the logical sequence of materials to be presented, the course, learning objectives, and outcomes that are suitable to those who will attend the training program.

The training environment is an important aspect of training effectiveness. When employees are attending a training session, several factors enhance or distract from their learning experience. These factors could be the space and colors of the building, seating arrangement, environmental considerations, the attitude of the employees, and other factors that may affect a positive learning environment. The key to establishing the best possible outcome is the leader. Leaders are role models, and they set the tone by their attitude, their passion, and interest for the job, and their relationship toward employees. Trainers set the stage for learning during training sessions to achieve the goals and objectives of training (Orey, 2014).

Training facilities may include auditoriums that are generally large-sized rooms, multiple purpose medium-sized instruction rooms, audio/visual-equipped rooms, and computer training rooms. A good training facility should have a flexible and technologically advanced learning environment. This means the environment may be able to adapt to new situations; and it must be safe, comfortable, and accessible. Another factor that may affect training effectiveness is training materials used by trainers. The main objective of using training materials is to involve the trainees during the activity, promote active interaction among them and encourage faster learning, and help improve their comprehension (Orey, 2014). These training materials are usually made up of video clips, audio, and hands-on tools to increase the learning experience of trainees. Training facilities should have high-quality indoor environments that can positively influence task performance and attention spans of trainees (Orey, 2014).

Another factor that may affect training effectiveness is the training schedule. The main goal is to motivate employees to be actively involved in the training program. This training schedule is designed to address relevant problems that may occur during training. Training schedules help find effective solutions to related contingencies that may arise during the training process (Silverman, 2015).

Presentation style is another factor that may affect training effectiveness from leaders to employees. The leader should be able to motivate employees and increase their desire to learn new ideas and skills. A presentation style helps employees learn as well as remember what they are being trained on. It could be as simple as a picture, video, power point, or acronym that draws the attention of employees. When planning a training session, it is wise that the leaders take their target audience (employees) into account. Think of it as marking and what type of audience would be interested in what is being sold. This could be achieved if leaders result in presentation styles that are lively and interesting (Silverman, 2015).

Summary of Section 1 and Transition

This study was conducted with a flexible design using qualitative methods specifically; a single case study design was used. This research is to seek the reason for the lack of effective training from leaders to employees resulting in decreased organizational performance. Qualitative research is broad and can possess exploratory aims. The methodology is unique in approach depending on the ontological and epistemological stance, but stems from the motivation to explore, seek understanding, and establish the meaning of experiences from the perspective of those involved (Mertens, 2008). Through the use of triangulation, this study overcame biases and provided the researcher with confidence in the findings. From a positivist viewpoint, there is one single reality, which is independent of the individual and can be studied and measured through relativist or interpreter's perspective.

The research framework is based on path-goal theory, transactional leadership theory, and transformational leadership theory with the concepts of leader engagement and leader time management. Leader time management includes providing employees with the appropriate knowledge and skills needed through training in order to produce optimal performance within an organization (Claessens, van Eerde, Rutte, & Roe, 2007). Figure 1 shows the relationship between the four elements associated with the research framework. With organizational performance as a foundation of the study, the researcher indicates that each element presented affects one another. It is the overall factor in whether employees are being effectively trained by their leaders.

This qualitative, single case study explores the impact of training on organizational performance within the government. The collected interview data from the government organization provided recommendations to improve organizational performance. It is the responsibility of leaders to ensure that their employees are competent and proficient in their performance. It is imperative that leaders effectively train their employees in order to develop the employees into future leaders within the organization. According to Low and Ang (2012), this improves employee retainability and has the tenancy to increase profit. Leaders that do not train effectively risk a lack of employee motivation, which can hinder recommendations for improvement and successful outcomes (Lindebaum & Zundel, 2013).

The specific problem to be addressed is the potential failure of leaders within government organizations, specifically Government organization to effectively train employees resulting in increased or decreased organizational performance. According to Higgins and Rowland (2005), effective leadership practices improve employee performance. When leadership practices are ineffective, employee performance is often difficult or nonexistent. Examples of ineffective leadership practices lack communication, listening, sharing information, and building interpersonal relationships with employees. According to Longenecker (2010), leaders are ineffective because they are stressed and burned out. This makes it difficult for leaders to effectively communicate, make decisions, or train employees adequately. Due to increased competition, globalization, changes in technology, politics, and the economy, leaders need to prepare employees for environmental changes

(Fernández-Esquinas, Pinto, Yruela, & Pereira, 2016). These changes enhance employee performance by promoting growth and career knowledge. Employees are an important resource for an organization and maximizing their contribution to goals helps in sustaining effective performance levels, which allows leaders to ensure that there are competent employees that are capable of developmental growth in their career field. Leaders have to assist their employees in obtaining the necessary skills through training in order to increase performance, commitment, and retention. A collection of characteristics in relation to specified events or behaviors are concepts (Brannick & Coghlan, 2016). Leader engagement and leader time management are the concepts of this study. It is the leader's responsibility to engage their employees in adequate training by providing clear directions and strategy in order to support business objectives. Leaders have to make time to adequately train employees. Without training, employees will not attain the knowledge and skills needed to perform their job (Claessens, van Eerde, Rutte, & Roe, 2007). Theories explain facts that have been widely tested and used to predict natural phenomena (Abend, 2008). The theories in this study are path-goal theory, transactional leadership theory, and transformational theory. Path-goal theory holds leaders accountable to fulfilling the needs of their employees. This theory suggests that leaders have a responsibility to plan and set goals to manage their time in order to train employees to attain proficiency. Transactional leadership theory states that leaders are concerned with structure and maintaining the status quo, which can decrease organizational performance. Employees are more likely not to receive training needed from their leaders in transactional leadership. However, leaders motivate their employees to pursue higher goals and are able to foster connection and innovation in transformational leadership theory (Peng, Liao, & Sun, 2020). The constructs of this study include training, organizational performance, and employee knowledge and skills. These constructs are building blocks to the theories that explain why the phenomenon behaves in a certain way.

The studies related to training suggest that training is not always effective and can be counterproductive. According to NG (2017), employees are not enthusiastic about training because it has become predictable and causes employees to disengage. The researcher suggests playing games such as Six Sigma will motivate and engage employees. Another study suggests that employees learn best as they go. The researcher believes that employee training is counterproductive and takes up valuable time instead of learning the process naturally (Eidt, 1992). The themes range from various techniques that could assist leaders when training employees. The themes are training contents, training environments, facilities and materials, training schedule, and presentation style. Various training methods help improve employee learning methods. These methods are taught by instructors, computer-based training, web-based training, and self-directed, interactive, or multimedia-inspired lessons. In addition, training environments and facilities enable a positive and flexible environment that encourages adequate training. It is also important to present the right material that will promote involvement and comprehension to employees (Orey, 2014). It increases employee learning experience. Leaders should provide their employees with a training schedule. This allows employees to ask any questions that they may have about the job or a specific task in order to perfect their performance. When in training, it is equally important how the leader presents the training to employees if they want them to remain interested. According to Silverman (2015), leaders motivate employees and increase their desire to learn and remember new ideas and skills through their training presentation style. Presenting the training session in a way that retains employee interest will encourage us to perform better in the future. Furthermore, it will spark leadership accountability in how they train employees. Perhaps leaders will be able to better manage their priorities to effectively training future leaders.

Chapter 8

The Research Project

Section 2: The Project

Research in leadership has largely focused on the traits and behaviors that make leaders and the leadership process more effective and constructive in organizational settings (Schaubroeck et al., 2007). However, there has been less attention on the traits that actually contribute to the ineffectiveness of leadership training. In order to examine the counter-perspective to the facilitating factors of leadership training, research has to be done to examine what contributes to the ineffectiveness of leaders to their employees. *The Leadership Quarterly* is a leading academic journal in leadership research published a special issue in 2007 that focused on destructive leadership (Harvey et al., 2007). However, according to the authors this study remains at an emerging stage in management and few studies have attempted to examine the factors that contribute to the ineffectiveness of project managers. Researchers argue that exploring the negativity of organizational behavior (Griffinand O'Leary-Kelly,

2004) and leadership (Popper, 2001), negative personal attributes of leadership can provide a more holistic view of how leadership can be ineffective (Burke,2006). In addition, such studies can also help in understanding how leadership effectiveness can be reduced by taking remedial measures to reduce factors that cause ineffectiveness of leadership training (Schaubroeck et al., 2007). Leadership training is a vital factor for success in organizational performance, and it is imperative to achieving the involvement and satisfaction from stakeholders (Schaubroeck et al., 2007). According to the researchers, a detailed examination of negative leadership attributes and organizational eliminations will help to improve the performance of leaders and raise the level of their training effectiveness. This research investigates the effects of training on organizational performance. In addition to the perceived effective behaviors and important leadership skills, negative attributes and organizational eliminations causing leaders to ineffectively train was also be studied. The goal of this research is to improve the understanding of factors that can undermine effective training to employees from leaders. The objective is to discover the personal attributes that make training from leaders effective or ineffective while identifying the factors affecting organizational performance from employees.

Purpose Statement

The purpose of this flexible single case study was to explore the impact of training on organizational performance within government. The research sought to determine gaps between the present performance of an employee or group of employees, and the desired performance. It was explored through an in-depth study of employee training from leaders and whether it leads to a high turnover of employees. The lack of effective training poses a threat to productivity and the overall performance of an organization. The success of an organization relies upon the performance of employees. According to Kozlowski (2012), effective training practices boost performance and develop the skills, knowledge, and expertise of employees and the organization.

Role of the Researcher

The role of the researcher in this study is to examine the training practices in organizations from leaders to employees and the effect it has on performances (Creswell & Miller, 2010). Qualitative methods of data collection that are flexible are used in interviews in which interviewees are given the floor to talk about their experiences and views. The interviewees were randomly sampled, which was guided by the researcher's need for information. The authors state that provisional analyses can change this need in which sampling takes place during the research and is interchanged with data collection. Contrary to probability sampling, which is based on the notion that the sample mathematically represented subgroups of the larger population, convenience sampling is aimed at being pure and straightforward with data (Creswell & Miller, 2000).

The researcher provided reliability and validity through gained valid knowledge about experiences or the culture of a specific individual or group in order to provide understanding and results of the specified study. An issue that can arise is the lack of control over the researchers' activities; therefore, researchers should keep detailed notes of their fieldwork, and the choices made in order to increase replication and reproducibility (Creswell & Miller, 2010). Quality procedures were developed, such as data triangulation and debriefing.

The significance of qualitative research is unified by the researcher's fundamental research question when they ask why? According to Creswell and Miller (2010), the research technique which the qualitative researcher uses is then to isolate and define phenomena during the process of research in order to comprehend and learn, whereas the quantitative researcher's ambition can determine the relationship between the phenomena already isolated and defined prior to the research.

According to Ashworth (1999), Bracketing is a method that can be used by some researchers in order to mitigate the potential effects of unacknowledged preconceptions or biases that are related to the research and increase the rigor of the project. The author states that sometimes the researcher may have a close relationship with the research topic which can cause preconceptions and biases. Both may precede and develop during the process of qualitative research. Bracketing is a method that protects the researcher from the cumulative effects of examining what may be emotionally challenging material. A lengthy research endeavor on an emotionally challenging topic can infuse the researcher with inherent challenges, become continuing research and, in turn, skew results and interpretations (Ashworth, 1999). Ashworth (1999) notes that bracketing can mitigate adverse effects of the research; importantly it also prompts the researcher to reach deeper levels of reflection across all stages of qualitative research. These stages are selecting a topic, population, designing the interview, collecting and interpreting data, and reporting the findings. By bracketing, the researcher acknowledged the challenges and tried to mitigate them. This was done by demonstrating the validity of the data collection and analysis process (Ahern, 1999). Therefore, efforts should be made by the researcher to put aside their preconception of knowledge, beliefs, values, and experiences in order to accurately describe participant experiences.

Summary

In this study, the researcher explored the impact of training on organizational performance within the government. It was explored through an in-depth study of employee training from leaders. Lack of effective training poses a threat to organizational productivity as well as performance (Kozlowski, 2012). The researcher's role was to examine training practices from leaders to employees in a single organization. The researcher used qualitative methods of data that are flexible through convenience sampling interviews. The significance of qualitative research is that it provides isolation and defines the phenomena in the study. According to Ashworth (1999), bracketing is a method used to mitigate biases related to the research. At times, the researcher can tend to feel an emotional connection to the research topic and develop preconceived notions that can have an effect on the validity of the researcher's study. In order to mitigate biases, the researcher has to acknowledge the challenges and validate the data collected by only recording participant experiences (Ahern, 1999).

Research Methodology

This study was conducted with a flexible design using qualitative methods specifically; a single case study design was used.   Qualitative research helps to gain insights into the phenomena in question and is flexible in the sense that it helps in identifying the missing part of what is unknown or partially known (Creswell, 2014). According to Creswell (2014) qualitative research is more relevant in the context of discovery and is able to attain access to what was not known previously. The study focused on the single case study approach as a research strategy. The single case study approach is an in-depth study or investigation of a contemporary phenomenon using a source of evidence within its real-life context (Lodico, Spaulding, & Voegtle, 2010). According to Lodico et al.

(2010), single case research is particularly useful when the phenomenon of interest is of a broad and complex nature and is best studied within the context in which it occurs. This study used explanatory research, which focuses on the factors that affect the relationships between training and organizational performance.

Discussion of Single Case Study

The appropriateness of a flexible design and a single case study is a desire to interpret and understand the experiences of people in a bounded system. A system is bounded when there is a person, group, program, or situation that can be investigated in order to gain understanding of experiences or views of the members of the system (Lodico et al., 2010). This study provides information on the researcher's positivism worldview and the methodology used to conduct research in an effort to seek answers to the research questions. Positivists are realists and believe that experience is important in determination rather than speculation (Brannick & Coghlan, 2016).

Discussion of Methods for Triangulation

Data triangulation is where the researcher interviews several groups for the verification of the findings and results. It is also referred to as cross examination. The appropriateness of data triangulation is to attempt to map out and explain the richness and complexity of human behavior by studying it from more than one standpoint (Kennedy, 2009). In using this approach, the researcher can be more confident by increasing the credibility and validity of the findings when different methods yield the same results (Kennedy, 2009). According to the author, when a researcher uses only one group, they just have to believe that the findings are correct; however, when a researcher employs more than one group to answer a single question, 2 out of the 3 may produce same results or all 3 of them may produce clashing results. In addition, the researchers then would either reframe the research question, reconsider the methods, or do both. The author also noted that the researcher would ultimately arrive at a more complete and wholesome picture of the phenomenon. Data triangulation provides a more detailed and balanced picture of the situation (Altrichter et al. 1996). The need to interview different groups in order to obtain conclusive results in qualitative research can be justified from the fact that qualitative researchers are generally interested in investigating the "why" and "how" aspects and a single method cannot explain every aspect of every phenomenon (Altrichter et al. 1996). The single questionnaire contained five demographic questions and nine interview process questions. In the first section of the questionnaire, the researcher collected demographic data to provide descriptive analysis for data triangulation purposes. This included the participant's age, gender, race, and how long they have worked for the organization. The second section of the in-person interview was the participants answering questions from the questionnaire. The collection of in-depth data for analysis was conducted by taking notes and asking follow-up questions that are based on what is revealed during the in-person interview. These questions are about the types of training being conducted. The interview questions helped the researcher collect information about how often the organization conduct training for the employees, whether the training increases productivity, performance, and skills, whether the training helps in task preparation, how employees conduct their own training, how much notice is given before training is conducted, and what are the training materials used.

These questions assisted in understanding the approaches, methods, and techniques of training within the organization.

Summary of Research Method

This study conducted with a flexible design using qualitative methods specifically; a single case study design was used. This research is to seek the reason for the lack of effective training from leaders to employees resulting in decreased organizational performance. Qualitative research is broad and can possess exploratory aims. The methodology is unique in approach depending on the ontological and epistemological stance, but stems from the motivation to explore, seek understanding, and establish the meaning of experiences from the perspective of those involved (Mertens, 2008). Through the use of data triangulation, this study overcame biases and provided the researcher with confidence in the findings. From a positivist viewpoint, there is one single reality, which is independent of the individual and can be studied and measured through relativist or interpreter's perspective.

Summary

The researcher explored the impact of training on organizational performance within the government. This was explored through an in-depth study of employee training from leaders. Lack of effective training can hinder organizational productivity as well as performance (Kozlowski, 2012). Examining training practices from leaders to employees in a single organization is the role of the researcher. The researcher used qualitative methods of data that are flexible through convenience sampling interviews. Qualitative research is significant because it provides isolation and defines the phenomena in the study. According to Ashworth (1999), bracketing is a method used to mitigate biases related to the research. The researcher may tend to feel an emotional connection to the research topic and develop preconceived notions that can have an effect on the research validity. This study conducted with a flexible design using qualitative methods specifically; a single case study design was used. This research seeks to find the reason for lack of effective training from leaders to employees resulting in decreased organizational performance. The approach of methodology depends on the ontological and epistemological stance, but stems from the motivation to explore, seek understanding, and establish the meaning from participant experiences (Mertens, 2008). Through the use of data triangulation, this study overcame biases as well as provide the researcher with confidence in the validity of the findings.

Participants

The participants of this qualitative single case flexible study were managers, supervisors, and employees from the organization. Information from the participants is essential in order to gain insight into training effectiveness (Lodico et al., 2010). Convenience sampling was employed in order to allow the selection of participants that are available to the researcher. Convenience sampling is defined as a method adopted by researchers where they collect market research data from a conveniently available pool of respondents (Hu & Qin, 2018). According to the researcher, for qualitative research, the intent is to obtain an in-depth understanding of a concept. Reporting information from a large group would present complex data to summarize due to the type of research being studied. According to Creswell and Plano Clark (2011), case studies generally have small participant group sizes that range from four to ten people. This allows for a more detailed analysis from the researcher. The researcher notes that, if possible, the data triangulation groups that have the necessary reliability can reproduce the potential ineffective features of the training within a particular process. The results of the research questions verified data triangulation which supports the processes within effective or ineffective training from leaders. Descriptive statistics are imperative when conducting qualitative research (Creswell & Plano, 2011). The interview consisted of an introductory part in the form of a permission request in addition to an in-person interview containing four demographic questions and nine interview questions.

Population and Sampling

In this section, the researcher described the population and sampling method. In qualitative research, a sample of the population is selected for any given study. According to Denzin and Lincoln (2000), sampling is the process where a researcher determines their sample. This is done by identifying the population of interest. The population is a group of people that the research is interested in making assumptions about (Denzin & Lincoln, 2000). The researcher determines the method of sampling as well as the sample size in order to perform quality research. The study's research objectives and the characteristics of the study population, size, and descriptive statistics determined which and how many people to select.

Discussion of Population

The researcher performed convenience sampling of Government organization managers, supervisors, and employees who range in ages between 17 and 65. Participants interviewed by the researcher using a single questionnaire. The in-person interview contained a total of 13 questions which included four demographic questions and nine questions pertaining to the types of training being conducted. It should take approximately 15-20 minutes per person to complete. Demographics such as education and race are not variables of this study. Familiarity with the interview participants is of limited concern. There were not any interview questions that delve into specifics about the organization that made the interviewee unwilling or uncomfortable about participation. This created an atmosphere that allowed them to speak freely. According to Creswell (2009), small participant research is considered normal in qualitative research.

Such small studies enable the researcher to gain a deeper understanding of participant experience and to develop a thick, rich description of that experience (Creswell, 2009).

Discussion of Sampling

In this study, the researcher performed convenience sampling. Convenience sampling is defined as a method adopted by researchers where they collect market research data from a conveniently available pool of respondents (Hu & Qin, 2018). According to Hu and Qin (2018), a convenience sample consists of participants that could be easily recruited in which data could be collected quickly because it is readily available. In this research, the sample included at least 20 participants and continued until saturation. According to Creswell and Poth (2018), the researcher should conduct 20 to 30 interviews based on field visits for collecting data until saturation is reached or there is no new information available. The researcher began with interviewing 23 participants and ended once saturation was achieved. Urquhart (2013) suggests that saturation is achieved when there is no new information that is learned from additional interviews. Saturation is defined as the state or process that occurs when no more of something can be absorbed, combined, or added (Urquhart, 2013). Saturation is an important aspect in qualitative research because it determines when there is enough data from a sample size from the study to develop a robust and valid understanding of the phenomenon. The participants in this study are conveniently selected within the ages of 20-65 years of age. The average length of time a participant has worked for the organization in a specific location is 0-6 years. The participants were selected in accordance with availability due to multiple work schedules. All of the workers within the organization are not able to be interviewed for the study because they may work a different shift or perform various tasks including assisting customers. In all forms of research, it would be ideal to test the entire population, but in most cases like this, the population is too large so that it is impossible to include every individual. This is the reason why most researchers rely on sampling techniques such as convenience sampling.

In terms of gaining access to the sample, the researcher has contacted the manager of the specified government organization via email. The manager has agreed to allow the researcher to interview participants for the study based upon availability. The researcher has also provided the manager with the DRP Permission Request form which can be found in the Appendix. The researcher provided a consent form to each participant in order to perform an ethical study because it solidified cooperation from participants and is used to communicate information and shared data.

Population and Sampling

The researcher of this qualitative single case flexible study interviewed 23 participants at Government organization until saturation was reached. These participants will meet the population of interest to the researcher. The populations of interest are managers, supervisors, and employees between the ages of 20 to 65 with approximately 0-6 years working at the organization. The manner of sampling was convenience sampling due to the large number of workers scheduled on various schedules. Convenience sampling is defined as a method adopted by researchers where they collect market research data from a conveniently available pool of respondents (Hu & Qin, 2018). It allows the researcher to obtain information from participants that is available during the specified time. During the interview, the researcher will provide participants with a single questionnaire containing 13 questions. The first section contained five questions pertaining to demographic statistics. The second section contained nine interview questions pertaining to training. For this study, the researcher made contact with the manager and provided a consent form to each participant in order to perform an ethical study. This form is imperative to gaining access to the sample and providing quality of research.

Data Collection

According to Creswell (2013), an in-person detailed in-depth interview is the most popular source of data collection in a qualitative case study. Yin (2012) notes in order to ensure a rigorous, comprehensive, and systematic research methodology the following must be done: preparation was made for data collection, collection of evidence, analysis of the evidence, and the composition of qualitative case study report. According to Gaya et al. (2013), the researcher must ask pertinent questions, listen attentively, adapt to unforeseen circumstances, grasp the issues being addressed, and identify and reduce effect of personal bias in the data collection process. The skill and personality of the researcher has a bearing in the qualitative case study research process and findings. In a qualitative single case study, rigorous data collection follows carefully linked steps, including in-depth interviewing of multiple sources in order to ensure consistent information (Gaya et al., 2013). Yin (2012) recommends the use of conceptual framework for the creation of case study databases in final reporting. This includes attaching study transcripts and the maintenance of evidence for data collection, data analysis, and discussion. The use of multiple sources of data enables the coverage of a broader range of views, issues, and facilitates triangulation of sources to reveal as much depth as possible while enhancing validity confirmation (Yin, 2012).

Data Collection Plan

The data collection plan began with the researcher interviewing participants based on convenience sampling. Convenience sampling is defined as a method adopted by researchers where they collect market research data from a conveniently available pool of respondents (Hu & Qin, 2018). This included Government organization managers, supervisors, and employees who range in age range between 17 and 65. Participants were interviewed by the researcher using a single questionnaire. It should take approximately 15-20 minutes per person to complete. The researcher interviewed an estimated population of 20 individuals that meet the criteria for this research study until saturation is met. The average length of time a participant has worked for the organization in the specific location is 0-6 years. The participants were selected in accordance to availability due to multiple work schedules. The single questionnaire contained five demographic questions and nine interview process questions. In the first section of the questionnaire, the researcher collected demographic data to provide descriptive analysis for data triangulation purposes. This included the participant's age, gender, race, and how long they have worked for the organization. The second section of the questionnaire is the interview guide, which asks questions about the types of training being conducted. The interview questions helped the researcher collect information about how often the organization conduct training for the employees, whether the training increases productivity, performance, and skills, whether the training helps in task preparation, how employees conduct their own training, how much notice is given before training is conducted, and what training materials are used. This is an appropriate plan for research because it allows the researcher to obtain pertinent data from participants that answer the questions needed. It can also provide a better understanding of how organization leadership practice is managed. Interviews are occasions for the researcher to learn something, not for them to teach or tell others what they think. The interviewee teaches the researcher about the inner workings of their organization.

Instruments

The interview guide lists questions that the researcher asked the participants during the interview (Oppenheim, 1992). The order of the questions and the level of degree to which is diverged from the defined list of questions were structured. In a structured interview, each participant was asked the exact same question in the same order. This type of interview is an effective approach with participants that are selected through convenient sampling. It is considered effective because the researcher does not know the background of the participants prior to the interview. According to the author, having a structured interview allows the researcher to ask the same question to participants, but obtain answers that are unique to the individual based on their personal experience. Having an interview guide is imperative in the qualitative interview process. How the researcher words the questions is key to the development of open-ended questions that are not leading (Oppenheim, 1992). The researcher used language that was suggestive, but participants were able to share their experiences or ideas without feeling as though the researcher wanted to hear a specific answer. Questions were straightforward and easy for the participant to understand in order to feel comfortable throughout the interview process.

The interview guide had basic demographic information that assessed individual participant background which assists in the researcher's analysis. This included the participant's age, gender, race, and how long they have worked for the organization. Additionally, this helped break the ice and make participants feel more comfortable. Then broader questions regarding the topic at hand were addressed. These questions began with the statement "What are/is", "How do", "Describe", and "Tell me". Using this type of language when creating the interview guide will help ensure that the right questions are being asked. These questions elicited more in-depth responses from each participant. The final question in the interview guide asked the participant if there is anything else that they would like to add. This question allowed the participant to share something that the researcher may not have directly asked in an earlier question or to share a thought that was relevant to an earlier question that they just realized.

All of the questions asked in the second section of the interview were focused on how each question addresses the research questions. The first questions are how often the organization conducts training for the employees and how much notice is given before training is conducted. These questions helped in answering why leaders fail to effectively train employees within an organization. The next set of questions describes how productivity is increased after training, what are the performance standards measured by, and what materials are used for training which helps answer the research question about how employees inhibit their own training. The final sets of questions are whether employees that are not skilled in specific departments work in those departments if needed and how often is job rotation. Those 13 questions answered what types of training are effective and what types are ineffective. This ensured that the data gathered is useful to the researcher. Not having a narrow focus for an interview study can cause the data gathered to be too general, which will be less effective in maximizing the end result. Having an interview guide ensured that questions lead to rich answers from participants, which will in turn lead to a more effective outcome (Oppenheim, 1992). The interview questionnaire can be referred to in the Appendix section.

Data Organization

For data organization to be effective, the researcher has to properly organize it for analysis. According to Stone-Romero (2002) recording an oral interview by writing down notes and recording on a recorder is wise. In addition, the researcher should maintain a spreadsheet in order to keep track of who is interviewed and at what time (Stone-Romero, 2002). This was very useful when the researcher input data from each interview. Once the researcher made a log of the participants numbers, they made sure the questions are well defined and transcribed in order to follow the flow of the chosen qualitative data collection method as closely as possible (Stone-Romero, 2002). When transcribing participant data, the researcher labeled and wrote a spreadsheet so that findings will be organized. Data organization was an appropriate process for the research project because having directories to information is an important aspect in data management. It saved the researcher time when locating data.

Summary of Data Collection

Having an in-depth interview that is in person is the most widely known source of data collection in a qualitative case study (Creswell, 2013). Yin (2012) notes that in order to ensure a rigorous, comprehensive, and systematic research methodology the following must be done: preparation was made for data collection, collection of evidence, analysis of the evidence, and the composition of qualitative case study report. In a qualitative single case study, rigorous data collection follows carefully linked steps, including in-depth face to face interviewing of managers, supervisors, and employees in order to ensure consistently of information from multiple sources (Gaya et al., 2013). The use of multiple sources of data enabled the coverage of a broader range of views, issues, and facilitates triangulation of sources to reveal as much depth as possible while enhancing validity confirmation (Yin, 2012). The data collection plan began with the researcher interviewing participants based on convenience sampling. Participants were interviewed by the researcher using a single questionnaire. The participants were selected in accordance with availability due to multiple work schedules. In the first section of the questionnaire, the researcher collected demographic data to provide descriptive analysis for data triangulation purposes. The second section of the questionnaire is the interview process which asked questions about the types of training being conducted. Having an interview guide assists in ensuring questions led to rich answers from participants, which led to a more effective outcome (Oppenheim, 1992). For data that are collected, it is important to organize it for analysis. The researcher should maintain a spreadsheet in order to keep track of who is interviewed and at what time. Setting up a recording device to record the entire interview so the researcher can focus on the session itself is wise; however, device recording was not approved by the organization. Data organization was an appropriate process because it saved the researcher time in locating data collected from participants.

Data Analysis

According to Watkins (2017), data analysis is the science of examining a set of data to draw conclusions about the information to be able to make decisions or simply to expand the knowledge on various subjects. It consists of subjecting data to operations. The author states that this is done to obtain precise conclusions that will help researchers achieve their objectives, such as operations that cannot be previously defined since data collection may reveal specific difficulties. Researchers perform data analysis in order to predict behavior trends and manipulate data, analyze the relationships, and correlations between data sets. Organizations can use data analysis to help identify the range of specific demographic groups which can provide insights into tweaking the issues such as training to better address employee needs.

Qualitative Analysis

Analyzing qualitative data is a process that is a rigorous and systematic interpretation of textual or visual data (Maxwell, 1996). Qualitative analysis can be consistent with themes and interconnections emerging from data presented. According to the author, repeatedly reading from the researcher yields new themes, connections, and deeper meanings from the first reading. Reading the full text of interviews multiple times before subdividing according to coded themes is imperative to appreciating the full context and flow of each interview before subdividing and extracting coded sections of text for separate analysis. According to Anderson (2003) coding is a common technique in qualitative analysis that involves developing codes for labeling sections of text for selective retrieval toward the end of analysis. Different approaches can be used for textual coding. One approach is structural coding which follows the structure of the interview guide. Another approach is thematic coding which labels common themes that appear across interviews through design of the topic guide or emerging themes assigned based on future analysis. In order to avoid the problem of code shifting over time, the researcher developed a standard codebook with written definitions and rules about when codes will begin and end. Codes that were developed and refined began to answer the original research questions. The author notes that it can facilitate that process through selective text retrieval when similarities within coding categories can be extracted and compared systematically. The standard practice is to write notes and record insights and patterns that emerge of the data and how they relate to the original research questions. Note taking is intended to entice further thinking about the data and initiate new connections that can lead to more coding and a deeper understanding (Anderson, 2003). In addition, analysis is dependent upon the thoroughness of the cross-examination and attempting to find alternative conclusions on the quality of the original conclusions. Cross-examining conclusions can occur in different ways. One way is using NVivo for qualitative data analysis. It is a computer software package that helps researchers organize, analyze and find insights in interviews, open-ended survey responses, journal articles, and media data. Another way is to encourage interaction between participants to challenge conclusions and pose alternative explanations for the same data. Anderson (2003) suggests that if alternative explanations for initial conclusions are more difficult to justify, confidence in those conclusions is strengthened.

Analysis of Triangulation

According to Burns and Grove (2001), data triangulation analyzing will involve the researcher examining data from different participants by using the same method. The researcher sought a pattern or contradictions beyond individual experience and considered the need to triangulate data collected from different groups of participants in order to show changes in experience. Because every method has a sort of bias to it, it is not uncommon that qualitative researchers collect data in different ways in order to build a better picture (Burns & Grove, 2001). The researcher performed data triangulation by interviewing different groups of participants and by collecting demographics information to perform descriptive analysis. In this study, the source of data collection is by recording the interviews in order to compare notes with the recording.

Summary of Data Analysis

Data analysis is referred to as the science of examining a set of data to draw conclusions about the information to be able to make decisions or expand the knowledge on various subjects (Watkins, 2017). It obtains precise conclusions that helped the researcher achieve set objectives that cannot be defined since data collection may reveal specific difficulties. The researcher performed data analysis in order to predict behavior trends and manipulate data and analyze the relationships between data sets. Analyzing qualitative data is a process that is a rigorous and systematic interpretation of textual or visual data (Maxwell, 1996). According to the author, repeatedly reading from the researcher yields new themes, connections, and deeper meanings from the first reading. In addition, coding is a common technique in qualitative analysis that involves developing codes for labeling sections of text for selective retrieval toward the end of analysis (Anderson, 2003). The structural approach allows for the use of the interview guide and the software NVivo. Thematic coding label's themes that are in cross based on further analysis that is needed. Codes that were developed and refined will begin to answer the original research questions. NVivo facilitated that process through selective text retrieval when similarities within coding categories can be extracted and compared systematically. According to Anderson (2003), note taking is intended to entice further thinking about the data and initiate new connections that can lead to more coding and deeper understanding. In addition, analysis is dependent upon the thoroughness of the cross-examination and attempting to find alternative conclusions on the quality of the original conclusions. Burns and Grove (2001) note that analyzing data triangulation will involve the researcher examining data from different participants using the same method. The researcher sought a pattern or contradictions beyond the individual experience and considered the need to triangulate between data collected at different times in order to show changes in participant experience. In this study, different groups of participants were interviewed and recorded. The different groups were managers, supervisors, and other employees. This was in the form of a quantitative survey in which participants ranked an experience or service, combined with a qualitative interview with open-ended questions.

Reliability and Validity

Reliability refers to consistency of certain measurements and the validity refers to whether those measurements measure what they are supposed to (Robson, 2002). However, in qualitative research reliability and validity are slightly different. Reliability in qualitative studies consists of being thorough, careful, and honest in carrying out the intended research (Robson, 2002). In qualitative interviews, this relates to practical aspects in the process of interviewing, to include the language of the interview questions, establishing rapport with the participants, and considering power relationship between the interviewer and the participant (Cohen et al., 2007). Validity seems more relevant when discussing qualitative research because there is often the issue of researcher bias, reactivity, and participant bias (Lincoln & Guba, 1985). Robson (2002) suggests that there are strategies aimed at addressing threats to validity, which are prolonged involvement, data triangulation, and participant debriefing.

Reliability

The researcher ensured reliability throughout the data collection process. When the data is collected it is important that the findings are precise, stable, and reproducible. The data was collected by the researcher conducting interviews in person of at least 20 participants until saturation is reached. Saturation is defined as the state or process that occurs when no more of something can be absorbed, combined, or added (Urquhart, 2013). This was achieved by the researcher applying methods consistently making sure to carry out the same steps in the same way for each measurement (Golafshani, 2003). Specifically for triangulation purposes, the researcher collected data to perform descriptive statistics during the in-person interview. The author states that this is ensured through the structured interview guide with prerecorded questions. During the interview process the researcher clearly defines how specific behaviors and responses were annotated and make sure questions are phrased the same way each time.

Validity

When ensuring validity, the researcher reflected the real variations as accurately as possible. According to Golafshani (2003), validity should be considered in the very earliest stages of research. Ensuring that the method and measurement technique are high quality and targeted to measure exactly what needs to be known. In this study, data collected on a questionnaire for training and were based on established theory and the questions were carefully and worded. The researcher used convenience sampling to select the participants. To produce valid results, clearly define the population being researched from a specific age range, geographical location, and organization (Golafshani, 2003). According to Birt et al. (2016), trustworthiness of results is imperative to qualitative research. Member checking is also referred to as participant validation, which provides credibility in results. The authors state that this is where the data collected is returned to participants in order to check for accuracy in experiences. It allows participants to engage with each other and add to the interpreted data following the structured interview (Birt et al., 2016). Ensuring that there are enough participants until saturation is reached was imperative to the research.

Bracketing

According to Ashworth (1999), sometimes the researcher may have a close relationship with the research topic which can cause preconceptions and biases. Both may precede and develop during the process of qualitative research. Bracketing is a method that protects the researcher from the cumulative effects of examining what may be emotionally challenging material. A lengthy research endeavor on an emotionally challenging topic can infuse the researcher with inherent challenges, become continuing research and, in turn, skew results and interpretations (Ashworth, 1999). According to the author, bracketing techniques employed by the researcher validated data collection and the analysis process. This is achieved through cross examination and putting aside preconceptions of knowledge, beliefs, values, and experiences in order to accurately describe participant experiences.

Summary of Reliability and Validity

In qualitative research, reliability consists of being thorough, careful, and honest in carrying out the intended research (Robson, 2002). Validity becomes an issue when there is researcher bias, reactivity, and participant bias present (Lincoln & Guba, 1985). Robson (2002) suggests that there are strategies aimed at addressing threats to validity, which are prolonged involvement, data triangulation, and participant debriefing. The researcher ensured reliability throughout the data collection process. This was achieved by the researcher applying methods consistently making sure to carry out the same steps in the same way for each measurement (Golafshani, 2003). When ensuring validity, the researcher reflected the real variations as accurately as possible. According to Golafshani (2003), validity should be considered in the very earliest stages of research. Ensuring that there are enough participants until saturation is reached was imperative to the research. Bracketing is a method that protects the researcher from the cumulative effects of examining what may be emotionally challenging material. The challenges that may be presented are skewed results and interpretations (Ashworth, 1999). According to the author, employing bracketing techniques validate the data collection and analysis process through cross examination and putting aside any preconception of knowledge, beliefs, values, and experiences in order to accurately describe the experiences of the participants.

Summary of Section 2 and Transition

The researcher explored the impact of training on organizational performance within the government. It was explored through an in-depth study of employee training from leaders. Lack of effective training poses a threat to organizational productivity as well as performance (Kozlowski, 2012). The researcher's role was to examine training practices from leaders to employees in a single organization. The researcher used qualitative methods of data that are flexible through convenience sampling interviews. According to Ashworth (1999), bracketing is a method used to mitigate biases related to the research. At times, the researcher can tend to feel an emotional connection to the research topic and develop preconceived notions that can influence the validity of the researcher's study. In order to mitigate biases, the researcher has to acknowledge the challenges and validate the data collected by only recording participant experiences (Ahern, 1999).

The researcher of this qualitative single case flexible study interviewed 20 or more participants at Government organization until saturation is reached. The populations of interest are managers, supervisors, and employees between the ages of 20 to 65 with approximately 0-6 years working at the organization. Convenience sampling was used due to the large number of workers scheduled on various schedules. Convenience sampling is defined as a method adopted by researchers where they collect market research data from a conveniently available pool of respondents (Hu & Qin, 2018). It allows for the researcher to obtain information from participants that is available during the specified time. During the interview, the researcher provided participants with a single questionnaire containing 13 questions. The first section contained five questions pertaining to demographic statistics. The second section contained nine interview questions pertaining to training.

Having an in-depth interview that is the most widely known source of data collection in a qualitative case study (Creswell, 2013). The use of multiple sources of data enabled the coverage of a broader range of views, issues, and facilitates triangulation of sources to reveal as much depth as possible while enhancing validity confirmation (Yin, 2012). The data collection plan began with the researcher interviewing participants based on convenience sampling. For data that are collected, it is important to organize it for analysis. The researcher should maintain a spreadsheet in order to keep track of who is interviewed and at what time. Setting up a recording device to record the entire interview so the researcher can focus on the session itself is wise. Data organization is an appropriate process because it saves the researcher time in locating data collected from participants. Data analysis is referred to as the science of examining a set of data to draw conclusions about the information to be able to make decisions or expand the knowledge on various subjects (Watkins, 2017). The researcher performed data analysis in order to predict behavior trends and manipulate data and analyze the relationships between data sets. Analyzing qualitative data is a process that is a rigorous and systematic interpretation of textual or visual data (Maxwell, 1996). Coding is a common technique in qualitative analysis that involves developing codes for labeling sections of text for selective retrieval toward the end of analysis (Anderson, 2003). The structural approach allows for the use of the interview guide and the software NVivo. NVivo can facilitate that process through selective text retrieval when similarities within coding categories can be extracted and compared systematically. Analysis is dependent upon the thoroughness of the cross-examination and attempting to find alternative conclusions on the quality of the original conclusions. Burns and Grove (2001) note that analyzing data triangulation involved the researcher examining data from different participants using the same method. According to the authors, the researchers can also design a mixed-method qualitative and quantitative study where very different methods are triangulated. This was in the form of a quantitative survey in which participants answered open-ended questions, and follow-up questions, and the researcher took notes.

In qualitative research, reliability consists of being thorough, careful, and honest in carrying out the intended research (Robson, 2002). Validity is an issue when there is researcher bias, reactivity, and participant bias present (Lincoln & Guba, 1985). The researcher ensured reliability throughout the data collection process. This was achieved by the researcher applying methods consistently making sure to carry out the same steps in the same way for each measurement (Golafshani, 2003). When ensuring validity, the researcher reflected the real variations as accurately as possible. According to Golafshani (2003), validity should be considered in the very earliest stages of research. Ensuring that there are enough participants until saturation is reached was imperative to the research. Employing bracketing techniques validate the data collection and analysis process through cross examination and putting aside any preconception of knowledge, beliefs, values, and experiences in order to accurately describe the experiences of the participants (Golafshani, 2003).

Chapter 9

Application to Practice

Section 3: Application to Professional Practice and Implications for Change

This section begins with an overview of the study. It provides a detailed discussion of the findings organized by themes discovered in the study with help from the software NVivo. The overview of the study provides a comprehensive analysis of the study that the researcher conducted. The results of these qualitative analyses include the theme triangulation with the research questions and research framework. The anticipated themes focus on differences, unanticipated themes, and themes that are missing. The literature review discusses how the findings relate with a focus on the similarities and differences. The application to professional practice discusses how the results can improve general leadership practice, potential implementation strategies, and recommendations for further study based on findings. Reflections discuss the researcher's personal and professional growth during the study. Lastly, the biblical perspective provided how the business functions integrate with a Christian worldview.

Overview of the Study

The purpose of this flexible single case study was to explore the impact of training on organizational performance within government organizations. The research design for this study included structured, in-person interviews and case study using an interview guided interviews to collect data. During a structured interview, each participant was asked the exact same question in the same order. This type of interview is an effective approach with participants that are selected through convenient sampling. It is considered effective because the researcher does not know the background of the participants prior to the interview (Oppenheim, 2018). According to the author, having a structured interview allows the researcher to ask the same question to participants, but obtain answers that are unique to the individual based on their personal experience. Having an interview guide is imperative in the qualitative interview process (Oppenheim, 2018). A private setting allowed participants a relaxed environment that was conducive to few interruptions.

In this study, participants verified data through respondent validation. The interviews involved providing the participants with the interview plan, asking questions, and closing the interview by thanking the participants and leaving the interview location. Numbers 1 through 23 replaced participant names. The following were the research questions in the study: How do leaders fail to effectively train employees within an organization, how do employees inhibit their own training, and what type of training are effective and what types are ineffective? The structured interviews of 23 respondents out of a total population of 163 employees in this government organization was the source of the data. The participants consisted of individuals with a minimum of 4 months of employment with the organization. Each participant consented to the organization's manager and agreed to be interviewed. The researcher ensured the accuracy of data by repeating participant responses, asking for more clarification, and asking to follow up questions. Participants were not comfortable with being recorded; however, detailed notes were approved, and they confirmed answers for clarification. The field notes enhanced all of the interviews. The researcher transcribed responses from the interviews and codes and themes created and evaluated data collected for prospective limitations and delimitations, identified implications for training, made recommendations for a follow-up study, and revealed introspective growth perceptions from the experience. The information and themes collected from the interviews provided a basis for understanding how organizational leaders may make decisions and develop strategies to adapt to the changing environments. The NVivo software allowed the researcher to organize large amounts of data and provide reliable data analysis (Hutchison et al., 2010). The research and evaluation methods integrated the problem statement, purpose statement, research question, and other elements of this study originally presented in Sections 1 and 2. The five themes emerged from the analysis of the data, and the recommendations involve leadership strategies and communication strategies.

Presentation of the Findings

The purpose of this qualitative single case study was to determine what methods of training, from leaders to employees, affect organizational performance. The research design for this study included 14 in-person interviews and 9 phone interviews that were structured. The structured interviews are open and provide new ideas discussed during the interview due to a participant's comments. A private setting in a conference room provided participants with a comfortable environment without interruptions. In this study, participants verified data through respondent validation. The interviews involved provided the participants with the interview plan, answering the 13 questions (5 demographic and 9 interviews), and closing out the interview with the 3 follow-up questions. The 3 follow-up questions were asked to gauge a better understanding of the interview questions. At the end, the researcher thanked participants for their time and assured them that their answers are anonymous. Numbers 1-23 replaced real names. The structured interviews were of 23 participants (5) managers, (4) supervisors, and (14) employees in this local government organization and were the source of the data. The participants consisted of individuals that were employed with the organization from 2 months to 20 years. The age groups ranged from 20-69 years old. Based on the sex of each individual, there were 34.78% males and 65.22% females. Each participant consented and agreed to the interview. The researcher completed each transcribed interview after once the follow-up questions were answered which ensured accurate data was detailed to gauge the knowledge and experiences. Field notes were taken on participant behavior during the process which provided a better understanding of how the participants generally felt about the questions being asked.

The transcribed responses from the interviews were analyzed using the software NVivo which produced codes and themes in order to organize the results of the study. The results for prospective limitations and delimitations implicated areas that lacked training. The information and themes that were revealed from the interviews provided a foundation for understanding how leaders within an organization could make decisions and develop strategies that adapt to the changing environment. NVivo assisted researchers in organizing the data and provided reliable data analysis (Hutchison et al., 2010). The research and evaluation methods integrated the problem statement, purpose statement, research questions, in addition to other elements of this study that were presented in Sections 1 and 2. Of all the data collected that were analyzed there were five themes that emerged.

Overview of Themes Discovered

The study discovered several themes related to the effects of training on organizational performance. The central theme is training practices. The presentation of findings (a) includes results that address the 3 research questions, (b) covers all the data, (c) relates the findings to include the conceptual framework and literature on effective training practices. The researcher established reliability by documenting all steps and ensuring the procedures were consistent and accurate throughout the study. The general goal of this process is to present findings that are valid and genuine (Marshall & Rossman, 2011). Establishing validity requires review of the transcribed data and validation from participants. In this study, the following was the central research question: How do leaders not effectively train employees within an organization? The two additional questions provided a detailed focus on the central question related to organizational performance. Researchers use triangulation methods in order to validate results. In this study, the researcher used data triangulation by examining data from different participants in order to seek patterns or contradictions beyond the individual experience and collected data at different times in order to show changes in participant experience. The different groups of participants were interviewed. The different groups consisted of managers, supervisors, and employees. This was in the form of a quantitative survey in which participants provided demographic information and open-ended questions. Using this method of triangulation decreased biases and validated the data. This particular government organization had outside companies that would come in to train leaders and employees depending on the specified task. In addition, employees could view certain training information using the internet. Internet searches have become extremely popular within the organization. The interview questions asked for on the survey included gaining information about policy and procedures, training guides, as well as organizational culture. Information regarding training policies and procedures varies depending on the department. It assisted in understanding the categorized decisions that were created to support administrative personnel functions, employee relations, and performance management. The establishment of policies can improve an organization's ability to meet requirements for training, and the management of employees. Moreover, it supported the emerging theme of feedback sources in the organization.

Discussion of Themes

The development of codes began after reviewing collected data and interviews through NVivo software. Keywords developed during the initial review of the data and included selected codes to the process of analysis after the first stage. The coding of information supported the development of emergent groups of similar data allowing for initial categorization of patterns (Neuman, 2011). The findings were organized by placing the data into clusters which in turn became themes. The results in this study addressed the central research question as well as factors and motivators in relation to organizational performance. Saturation began at participant 17 and extended to the point of replication. The researcher verified this further through the data analysis process. Each participant was asked to elaborate on specific occurrences that were brought up by them or mentioned by previous participants. In addition, the researcher read back the questions and participant answers to ensure accurate information was transcribed. Through a process of repeated and prolonged data analysis, it was determined that there were five themes from this study. The themes were (a) organizational culture, (b) leader and employee engagement, (c) organizational resources, (d) training practices, and (e) leadership challenges. The themes that emerged are significant factors that influence organizational performance practices. The significance of exploring the effects of training on organizational performance may assist leaders with implementing practices in order to increase productivity, profitability, and reduce turnover rates allowing leaders to sustain organizational development.

Table 2: Distribution of Respondents Based on Role

Role	Total	Percentage
Manager	5	21.73
Supervisor	4	17.39
Employee	14	60.88
Grand Total	**23**	**100**

Table 2 represents the profile of the respondents in terms of their role. There are 5 respondents, 21.73%, who are in the role of manager, 4 respondents, 17.39% who have the role of supervisor, and 14 employees which make up 60.88% of the 23 participants. The data implies that majority of the respondents are employees, which means that the people who comprise the workforce within this organization are very impressionable and present a good reflection on their training experiences with leaders and how it affects their overall performance.

Table 3: Distribution of Respondents Based on Age Group

Age Group	Total	Percentage
20-29	4	17.39
30-39	5	21.73
40-49	4	17.39
50-59	6	26.1
60-69	4	17.39
Grand Total	**23**	**100**

Table 3 represents the profile of the 23 respondents in terms of their age. There are 4 respondents, 17.39%, who are in the age range of 20-29 years old. Five respondents, 21.73%, whose ages are 30-39 years old. Four respondents, 17.39, are in the age range of 40-49. There are 6 respondents, 26.1% who are in the age range of 50-59 years old and 4 respondents, 17.39% within the age of 60-69 years of age. The data imply that majority of the respondents are in the age range of 50-59 years old.

Table 4: Distribution of Respondents Based on Sex

Sex	Total	Percentage
Male	8	34.78
Female	15	65.22
Grand Total	**23**	**100**

Table 4 presents the profile of the respondents in terms of their sex. There are 8 respondents, 34.78%, who are male. There are 15 respondents, 65.22% who are female. The data show that majority of the respondents are female within the organization.

Table 5: Distribution of Respondents Based on Race

Race	Total	Percentage
White	15	65.22
Latino	2	8.71
Black	5	21.73
Asian	1	4.34
Grand Total	**23**	**100**

Table 5 presents the profile of the respondents based on their race. There are 15 respondents, 65.22%, who are white. Two respondents or 8.71% are Latino, 5 respondents or 21.73% are black, and 1 respondent or 4.34% is Asian. The data implies that majority of the respondents are white.

Table 6: Distribution of Respondents Based on Years of Service Within Organization

Years of Service Within Organization	Total	Percentage
0 to 4	7	30.44
5 to 9	5	21.73
10 to 14	6	26.1
15 to 19	4	17.39
20 to 24	1	4.34
Grand Total	23	100

Table 6 presents the profile of the respondents based on their year in service working for the organization. There are 7 respondents, 30.44%, who have worked within this particular organization for 0-4 years. Five respondents make up 21.73% that have worked for the organization for 5-9 years. There are 6 respondents, 26.1%, that have worked for the organization for 10-14 years. Four respondents, 17.39%, make up for the 15-19 years of service while 1 respondent, 4.34%, represents 20-24 years within the organization. The data implies that majority of the respondents have worked in this government organization for 0-4 years, which coincides with the high employee turnover rate.

Theme 1: Culture

The first theme of this study is organizational culture. Characterizing the culture within an organization is important. Fostering a positive, supportive, encouraging environment where employee morale is high has a huge impact on employee motivation. Beheshtifar and Nazarian (2013) noted employees who do not feel connected exhibit dissatisfaction through withdrawal behaviors such as a reduction in productivity, absenteeism, low employee morale, and high turnover rates. Kavitha, Geetha, and Arunachalam (2011) conducted a study on employee retention to examine the factors that influence turnover. Using the method of convenience sampling, a sample size of 23 participants provided the research data. The results indicated communication, job satisfaction, and training influenced performance and turnover rates. For example, an increase in employee turnover rates may have a negative effect on employee motivation. When employees become dissatisfied with their job, employee turnover increases (Galletta et al., 2011). The researcher interviewed each participant by asking them

13 questions. The first section was (5) demographic and the second section were an interview guide with 9 questions. Participants were then asked follow-up questions to provide which were transcribed by the researcher. In the transcript excerpts, participants received anonymity using numbers (Participants 1-23) not representing any part of their name or specific department within the organization.

The transcribed excerpts that support the findings on the organizational culture are as follows: "Daily turnover rate is high" (Participants 10, manager and 23, employee). In addition, when the researcher asks participant 23 why the turnover rate was so high, the participant states "The on-boarding process is lacking and requires revamping. Participant 13 agreed to the interview but appeared to be frustrated with the culture of their specific department within the organization. Their direct quote was "The work environment is very poor". When the researcher asked the participant to elaborate on this answer, they state "There are a lot of older people working within specific departments and want to stick to the status quo. They are not willing to conform to new rules and regulations in regard to tasks. They feel that their way is the best way and that is frustrating". In addition, this same participant mentions the high employee turnover within the organization. Participant 22 says, "We have a laid-back work environment, but professional even though I work behind the scenes with customers". Not all participants gave negative views as noted above. Most of the participants had very positive things to say about the organization's culture such as Participant 1 (manager), who states, "This organization makes me smile". Participant 7 suggests, "The environment where I work is very engaging and empowering". Participant 15 asserts, "The organization is a great place to work". The results in this study revealed that 82.60% of participants had a positive attitude about the organizational culture.

Theme 2: Engagement

The second theme identified is engagement. Participants provided data by addressing question 3 "How do employees conduct their own training?" on the interview questionnaire. This question led to additional questioning from the researcher based on some of the participant responses. Some of the participant responses addressed leaders being too busy to participate in training and rarely engage with employees. Dezso and Ross (2012) noted that the behavior and performance of employees were largely a function of organizational leaders that determine an organization's strategic and organizational decisions. Leaders are in an ideal position in which they detect and investigate effects in the organization that can potentially hinder performance in the organizations (Ruark, 2010). Information that is transmitted by leaders has a powerful influence on employees' interpretations of their work experiences (Yiwen, Lepine, Buckman, & Feng, 2014). Mollick (2012) states that leadership in organizations had a large impact on the performance of employees. Participant 3 describes leader and employee engagement within their department as "A few times a year". Participant 12 states, "Rare because our job is busy and morale is lowered". Participant 21 (employee) states that the "Lack of engagement between leaders and employees create barriers". On the other hand, participant 10 (manager) describes engagement as "Daily meetings where the employees have the opportunity to speak freely and leaders listen to concerns. There is a good report and have an open relationship". Participant 14 (manager) answers "Leaders regularly engage with employees". Similarly, participant 18 states "Every day we are all encouraged and stay positive". A positive work environment can lead employees to have higher levels of effort in support of the goals and strategies of the organization (Allen, Ericksen & Collins, 2013). Moreover, active engagement contributes to building employee decisions skills, and they are more willing to contribute their skills on behalf of the organization. A positive environment reduces emotional fatigue and job-related stress, both of which positively relate to turnover rates in organizations. As employees feel that they have influence in their specific department and overall organization, they are less likely to seek alternative employment arrangements which will reduce turnover (Allen, Ericksen & Collins, 2013).

Table 7: Distribution of Respondents Based on Leaders Readily Available to Train

Employees Conduct Own Training	Total	Percentage
Leaders available when needed	11	45.82
Don't usually get training/No	2	10.73
Only on Zoom conferences now	1	4.34
Sent to other departments or organizations	3	13.04
Employees seek out online/webinars/train each other	6	26.07
Grand Total	**23**	**100**

Table 7 presents data collected from respondents answering the question is readily available to train leaders. There were 11 respondents, 45.82%, who answered that leaders are available when needed. Two respondents, 10.73%, answered they do not usually get training or no. One respondent, 4.34%, answered they are only on zoom conferences for training. Three respondents, 13.04% answered sent to other departments or organizations. Additionally, 6 respondents, 26.07% answered that employees seek out online training, webinars, or employees train each other. The data suggests that the majority of leaders are readily available to train employees.

Theme 3: Resources

The third theme in the study is resources. Participants provided data on the resources by answering question (3) "How do employees conduct their own training?", (4) "What are the training materials used for training?", and for more clarification (RQ2) "How do employees inhibit their own training?". The resources that are available within the organization vary. Most of the resources available to participants are directed to Google or online training systems if there is a question or task that needs to be answered. When the researcher asks participant 13 (manager) to elaborate, the participant states "I went to Human Resources a week ago about a specific question and they still have not followed up with me. I'll probably go there after this interview and I'm sure they're still not going to have an answer for me".

Performance Measurements. Organizations have sought ways to improve the performance of workers, and scholars have developed and tested theories to predict performance in work environments. There are differences among theories, but the consensus is that leadership strategies are vital for improving organizational performance (Cailler, 2014). According to the author, effective leaders have a positive effect on employee training following feedback. Participants were asked to answer question 6 "What are the performance standards?". The participant responses were as follows: Participant 6 responds, "Performance standards are measured by the timely and accuracy of performing tasks. This is not to punish or degrade, but to understand where additional training is needed". Also, participant 14 who is a manager says, "Performance standards are measured by tasks being able to be completed independently and accurately". Moreover, participant 16 states, "They are measured by your job performance". All of the participants in this study were aware that performance measurements were based on revenue goals set by local government counsel and directors shown by the following comments: Participant 9 responds, "Goals that are outlined by counsel and directors which are met within the organization annually". Participant 1 states, "Making sure requests are completed and there is adequate revenue coming in". Participant 12 asserts, "Performance relates to incoming revenues and how well employees complete their tasks based on yearly performance reports". Additionally, when Participant 1 answers question 6, they answered "Please see our Excellence Distinction".   There were 31.13% of participants who had positive responses to the organization's performance standards. Only 4.34% of the participants note negative responses about the performance standards by stating the following: Participant 13 exclaims, "Mostly by how much someone likes the employee, not performance". Participant 19 (employee) says that they were "unsure" about performance standards. Participant 20 asserts, "Training is not a requirement in performance standard". Participant 22 exclaims, "Everything is based upon on revenue and customer complaints because we cater to our residence".   A system that does not have adequate feedback mechanisms is out of control (Smith, 2009). There is evidence that the practice of performance measurement exists with feedback. Performance feedback is in place as further shown by the following responses. Participant 2 remarks, "We have measurable standards and steps to achieve". Participant 4 mentions, "We have an annual performance review where clear goals for the past year are analyzed for progress. New goals for the upcoming year are naturally set with encouragement and direction from our supervisor". Participant 5 asserts, "We have reviews – self/manager". Participant 8 says, "We only have goals set by the department". Taylor (2014) stated that there are empirical studies that have shown instances where the actual behavioral outcomes contradicted the desired behavioral outcomes of performance management due to different desires of employees. Organizations consist of different individuals and groups who have different aspirations, goals, and views. However, using elements such as incentives, positive feedback, and improved decision making may shape more positive behaviors and performance by employees.

Tools/Materials. Van De Mieroop and Vrolix (2014) noted that leaders within an organization are constantly using performance appraisal strategies as a tool in order to improve competencies. Providing tools and resources to employees are tasks that have to be accomplished in order to complete a task. Employees cannot meet performance requirements without them. It can be physical items such as having access to technology or comparable to content knowledge. Resources are the places where employees can go to for assistance with training, financial resources, or other information. The findings indicated 80% of participants believed having the resources to perform the job increased performance. Additionally, 10% of participants believed that having inadequate resources to perform the job makes employees dissatisfied. Furthermore, 10% of participants believed that providing effective resources to do the job can improve. Participant responses are as follows: Participant 3 suggests, "There may be a need for training to help us understand where to look online for tools". Participant 5 exclaims, "We already have books, but no one really utilizes them". Participant 7 states, "Accustomed to be self-sufficient, look through Google, or asking co-workers for help. There is not official guide to look at for help". Participant 22 states "We are encouraged to be proactive which means we just have to look around and resources".

Theme 4: Training Practices

The fourth theme of this study is training practices. The results of training practices in this study vary in accordance with the specific department within the organization. They were also placed into categories of effective and ineffective. Collier, Green, and Peirson (2011) noted that organizations have the ability to sustain growth when leaders effectively train employees than organizations that do not train effectively. The data analyzed that only 7% of participants had positive experiences when it came to training. Ninety-three percent of participants experienced the latter. Some of the responses were as follows: Participant 1 asserts, "Monthly lunch and learn sometimes not the best because we go mainly for lunch. We also often criticize the speakers/instructors". Participant 6 suggests, "Limited training to go and not allowing people to attend training because it is not required". In addition, participant 6 notes "Felt that I had to educate myself because we have different agencies train us on how to perform our job". Participant 5 states, "They don't provide high level training. Training in my department is generally sink or swim by leaders". Participant 8 suggests, "Open to training, but leaders need to understand specific departments they are training. Not everyone needs the same training. Recognition is a way to understand that trainers are skilled". Participant 11 (supervisor) exclaims, "A lot of people that has been there for a long time and have institutional knowledge and unwilling to change, delegate, or share knowledge. There are also no guides for specific tasks. They only shadow employees". Participant 12 (supervisor) states "Training is good but feels pushed and leaders do not listen. I feel that leaders need to engage with employees because the lack of communication makes employees feel pushed to do training that is unwanted. When I first started, there was no training from managers as far as what to expect on the job". Participant 13 (manager) responds, "Weak leadership, no integrity, no strength of character. Management is panicked and training is not a priority toward excellence. My department specifically is that you learn by discovery, not by orientation. Employee manual not discussed, not gone over". Additionally, Participant 13 adds "You see people to develop them. Many employees want to just do their job specific tasks. If employees don't get recognized, they give up. Managers are not showing employees' growth toward excellence. No one wants to allow employees to grow. No orientation or guides from Human Resources".

Participant 15 states, "Should give a little bit of training". Participant 17(manager) suggests, "An official manual with benchmarks would be helpful". Training and quality decisions affect the profitability of organizations. In addition, taking time to develop career paths and learning opportunities within an organization will keep employees engaged and ensure the next level of leadership is developed proactively (Ross, 2012).

Table 8: Distribution of Respondents Based on How Often Training is Conducted

How often training is conducted	Total	Percentage
Often	4	17.39
Monthly	3	13.07
Quarterly	2	8.69
Semi-Annually	4	17.39
Annually	5	21.73
Maybe 1-2 times per year/As needed	5	21.73
Grand Total	**23**	**100**

Table 8 presents data collected from respondents answering the question of how often training is conducted. There were 4 respondents, 17.39%, who answered that training was conducted often. Three respondents, 13.07% answered monthly. Two respondents, 8.69%, answered quarterly. Four respondents, 17.39%, answered semi-annually. Five respondents, 21.73% answered annually and an additional 5 respondents, 21.73% answered maybe 1-2 times per year. The data implies that majority of the respondents are trained at least once annually by leaders.

Table 9: Distribution of Respondents Based on How Much Notice is Provided Before Training

Notice provided before training	Total	Percentage
Year in advance	2	8.69
1-2 Months in advance	8	34.78
A week	9	39.13
None/Rarely	4	17.4
Grand Total	**23**	**100**

Table 9 presents data collected from respondents answering the question of how much notice is provided before training occurs. There were 2 respondents, 8.69% answered a year in advance. Eight respondents, 34.78%, answered 1-2 months in advance. Nine respondents, 39.13%, answered a week in advance.

Four respondents, 17.4% answered none or rarely. The data implies that majority of the respondents receive notice for training at least a week prior.

Notice provided before training. Stating the kind of training that will be offered, for whom, the day, date, time, and location is imperative. It is also important to let employees know if the specified training is mandatory or voluntary. Explaining what the training will consist of, how it can benefit each employee, and what is needed to prepare for the training is crucial. In the questionnaire, question 2 "Describe how much notice is given before training is conducted?" allowed for the participants to provide responses. Some of responses were as follows: Participant 1 (manager) states, "It depends on the training opportunity. Our annual conferences are known a year in advance". Participant 4 states "Last time we had internal organized training was for our software 7-9 years ago and we were very much involved from the beginning, including rating the vendors who responded to RFP. Therefore, we easily had 1 year notice. We do have a department retreat annually (months of notice) where we spend 2-3 days delving into goals, objectives, entire department tasks, etc.". Participant 10 (manager) says, "We give 3 notices…verbal, text, and in morning meeting. Sometimes 1 month in advance or 1 week in advance". Participant 12 (supervisor) suggests, "One month for Lunch and Learn then for specific training it is about 4 months prior". Participant 13 (manager) states, "Notice is provided one week in advance…Sometimes". Participant 14 notes "Usually, formal training about a week is given. On the job is spur of the moment". The consensus of this question was that 82.6% (managers, supervisors, employees) believe that notice is provided in an acceptable about of time prior to training in all departments within the organization.

Job Rotation. Job rotation is in place to help employees learn different functions within their department. It increases the variety of tasks and physical demands that are required for the job. The objective is to provide a consistent and systematic method of developing formal job rotations that are based on the requirements of the jobs. Questions 7 and 8 on the Interview guide asked, "How often is job rotation" and "Do employees that are not skilled in specific departments work in those departments if needed?" Data proved that 60.87% (3 managers and 11 employees) of participants have job rotation within their departments while 39.13% (2 managers, 3 supervisors, and 4 employees) of participants do not. Of the departments that do job rotation, the responses were: Participant 4 says, "For those cross-trained, certain tasks can be spread out to those available, in case the usual person is busy with a project". Participant 6 answers, "Job rotation is performed daily or weekly. Although an employee is not highly skilled in a specific department they still work there. I try to find tasks and duties that complement their skill set".

Increase of productivity after training.
Question 5 asked the 23 participants to "Describe how productivity is increased after training?". Only 16.39% of participants shared negative feelings in their responses. At the time this question was being answered in-person, the researcher notes that Participant 13's (manager) behavior was disgruntled, but very open about their feelings toward their workplace and the people in it. When answering the question, the participant responds with "Very poor-there is very little training, no accountability, and no personal growth-development plan". However, 83.61% of participants stated the following Participant 6 (employee) suggests, "Productivity has increased by an employee's ability to perform the tasks efficiently.

What I noticed is that now employees are able to grasp an understanding of the job faster". Participant 14 (manager) says, "Individuals are more confident and competent. A difference is noticed as the individual is able to work more independently". Participant 20 (employee) exclaims, "Yes. Trained then I have more knowledge which proves clarity".

Effective and Ineffective Training. Effective training helps employees improve their competence, capacity, and performance as well as gain a new perspective on knowledge and skillset. Having data on what types of training are effective and ineffective to the organizations helps avoid the unnecessary costs that come with training if it is not helpful. The researcher asked participants RQ3 for more clarification. The research question was "What types of training are effective and what types are ineffective?". Specific training mentioned by participants was Lunch and Learn and the 5 Voices training. The Lunch and Learn varied in responses. Although the responses were positive and boosted morale, the maximum participation was because it offered free food. Some of the responses were that participant 7 (employee) answers, "Lunch and Learn boosts morale and is very interactive". Participant 21 (employee) states,

"Effective, but sometimes the information goes in one ear and out the other if the speaker just shows slides and there is no interaction". The 5 Voices training was found to be the most popular with all 23 participants. What constituted as effective training was training that is led by specialist in specific field, training that is engaging with visuals, and hands-on. Participant 12 (supervisor) says, "Engage with people not just to talk. Want participants to do in-person hands on training". Participant 6 (employee) responds, "Visual training that is written down and shown. It also helps to have manuals to reference". Moreover, participant 18 says "Rather be in class or in-person than online to answer any question that I have. I like to be able to network, and info share with others". The types of training that constituted as ineffective for 91.30% of participants were training that was telling and not showing how to perform specific tasks. One participant stated "When it comes to training, I was told to look through my notes and I have to figure it out because I was trained on it before. That doesn't help me if I was trained months ago and don't really understand what I am looking for. Participant 5 answered, "It's frustrating". Participant 8 (supervisor) states, "Training that is mandatory tends to be biased. Seems to be less fun". Participant 19 (employee) remarks, "Online training is not retained be there is no real-world application. Most of the training is just click through until you get the right answer".

Theme 5: Leadership Challenges

The fifth theme that was identified was Leadership Challenges. Employees provided data by addressing RQ1 "How do leaders fail to effectively train employees within an organization?". Leadership challenges are important to identify because they can provide opportunities to grow and develop personally and professionally. When faced with a challenge, leaders have to seek out ways to overcome that challenge in order to progress in their career or personal life. It builds self-confidence, which instills self-trust and to be able to face and overcome the challenges that may arise in the future. Furthermore, overcoming leadership challenges can enhance a leader's skillset because they may be required to learn new skills in order to conquer the challenge. The data revealed 94% of participants mentioned what they felt needed to change. Participant 19 (employee) responds, "Organizational change provides good notes, but the leaders do not answer employee questions. We are always told to refer to our notes". Participant 20 (manager) states, "The organization can use better on boarding for new hires in my experience. They are hiring people that should not be in a position to perform specific skills, which is why there is a high turnover rate here. My manager is unmotivated which makes me unmotivated to even want to learn". Participant 3 (employee) exclaims, "My supervisor does not know their job, so it is not productive when they try to train me or other co-workers". Participant 22 (employee) remarks, "Try to make training important because it seems to get put on the back burner at times since they are always busy or forget. It seems as though I am alone and have to ask others for assistance even though we do different jobs within my department".

Relationship of Findings to Research Questions

The three research questions were the primary basis for collection of data and analysis within the study. Efforts in data collection were performed in order to ensure that there was adequate information that supported and strengthened the researcher's purpose of study. During the interview, the researcher asked the participants each of the three research questions in an effort to gain further understanding.

Relationship of Findings to Research Framework

The Research Framework contributes to the study in two ways because it (1) identifies research variables, and (2) clarifies relationships among the variables. It is linked to the problem statement, the conceptual framework and sets the foundation for the presentation of the three research questions. The research questions drive the investigation being studied.

Concepts

A concept is the process of classifying and categorizing objects or events that have common characteristics beyond any single observation (Brannick & Coghlan, 2016). The researcher abstracts the meanings from experiences and use words as labels to designate them then designs the hypotheses using concepts. The researcher then devises measurement concepts by which to test these hypothetical statements and collect data using the measurement concepts. The concepts that are discussed in this research are leader engagement and leader time management.

Leader Engagement. The findings relate to Leader engagement because it is the responsibility of the leader to educate the employees by clearly identifying the path for growth (Mendes & Stander, 2011). Information that is transmitted by leaders has a powerful influence on employees' interpretations of their work experiences (Yiwen, Lepine, Buckman, & Feng, 2014). This is performed through the engagement of training employees in order to support strategic business objectives and meet the common needs. Employee knowledge and skills are impacted through implementing path-goal theory and leader engagement. Leader engagement is connected to effective training for employees by building and strengthening relationships.

Leader Time Management. Leader time management relates to the themes of engagement, training practices, and leadership challenges because there have been statements transcribed by participants that leaders have put other things as a priority instead of training employees as needed. Employees were often told to refer to their notes from the past instead of helping the employee to understand the specific task or process when asked. Leader time management is a process of planning and exercising time that is spent on specific activities, especially to increase effectiveness, efficiency, and productivity (Claessens, van Eerde, Rutte & Roe, 2007).

RQ1. *How do leaders fail to effectively train employees within an organization?* The theme that was resonated with this research question were: (d) training practices and (e) leadership challenges. Training practices and leadership challenges were themes prevalent in this research question because statements made from participants indicated that lack of communication and training from leaders were not helpful to their growth and development. In training practices an astounding 83% of participants were dissatisfied with the training methods displayed by leaders. In regard to leadership challenges 92% responded to this research question with statement of where they felt that their leader failed at. Participant 21 (employee) states, "Lack of engagement between leaders and employees create barriers". Participant 6 (employee) says, "Limited training to go and not allowing people to attend training because it is not required". Participant 5 (employee) exclaims, "Felt that I had to educate myself because we have different agencies train us on how to perform our job. They don't provide high level training. Training in my department is generally sink or swim by leaders". Participant 22 (employee) states, "Try to make training important because it seems to get put on the back burner at times since they are always busy or forget. It seems as though I am alone and have to ask others for assistance even though we do different jobs within my department". The researcher believes that it is imperative that leaders gauge with their employees often to find out what is working and what is not working in their work relationship. Building relationships and providing feedback that is often instead of the once-a-year scheduled timing can have a huge influence on employees. Also, the "one size glove" term does not fit all. Individuals learn in different ways, and it is not up to the leader to determine how an individual learns. The leader has to take strides to alter how they instruct/teach others in a way that is beneficial for that individual. The fact that there is a high percentage of participants that indicated there is a training issue within the organization is the first step in identifying the problem.

RQ2. How do employees inhibit their own training? The themes that were prevalent to this research question were: (a) leader and employee engagement, (b) organizational resources, and (c) training practices. Leader and employee engagement stand out as a number one issue when it comes to this research question. Employees will have a hard time communicating their needs to leaders if they feel as though the relationship is lacking empathy and trust which is common behaviors of communication barriers. When there is a communication barrier present or the leader does not have time to engage in training of their employee, employees have to rely on themselves. While taking the initiative to study and brush up on skills individually is highly encouraged and beneficial, there are instances where employees feel as though there is just not enough understanding and assistance from a leader is needed to fill those learning gaps. During the interview process, 30.43% of participants described their engagement with leaders as Participant 12, supervisor) "Rare" and (Participant 21, employee) "Lack of engagement between leaders and employees create barriers". The fact that the first statement was coming from a supervisor indicates that this behavior is not just between an employee and their supervisor, but perhaps the supervisor and manager as well.

The second theme that resonated with Research Question 2 was organizational resources. This theme was very disturbing to know that there was a lack of resources within a government agency that was geared toward providing resources for their own residents. Participants answered the interview question (4) "What are the training materials used for training?". Eighty-three percent of participants stated that "We have books, but we don't use them", "I went to Human Resources a week ago about a specific question and they still have not followed up with me. I'll probably go there after this interview and I'm sure they're still not going to have an answer for me". The participants had issues with obtaining resources from Human Resources in addition to always being referred to seeking information from outside vendors that were involved in their training processes because they were more knowledgeable. It seems as though there is a lack of subject matter experts (SME) that are skills to train in specific areas located within the organization, which is not very cost effective. In fact, participant 7 (employee) says, "Other positions are not knowledgeable for training everyone, so we have outside vendors which is not cost effective". In addition, 32% are often told to look up training material/tools through Google or online webinars. Participant 11 (supervisor) states, "We don't use material to train only if you are a new hire. We have to rely on Google for updated information".

The third theme is training practices. Training notices were consistent in all participants responding to adequate notice provided from leaders even though training is conducted in sparse timing depending on the department. The data analyzed showed that 69.56% of participants associated training as a negative experience. Participant 21 (employee) exclaims, "Leaders do not listen to employees or intake the innovation on performing in a more efficient way". In addition, in a conversation the researcher had with the government organization's city manager, the manager states "Our training programs need to be a lot better which is another reason why we have high turnover".

RQ3. What types of training are effective and what types are ineffective? The themes highlighted in this research question are all five themes (a) organizational culture, (b) leader and employee engagement, (c) organizational resources, (d) training practices, and (e) leadership challenges. The researcher found that the findings suggest that the culmination of the organizational culture, which is laid back, although friendly, leaders have a sense of conducting their training on their own time when beneficial to them individually. This affects engagement behaviors, which a big portion of that is generally offered when training is conducted in a mass setting. In this case there is max participation because they are offered an incentive such as free lunch. Although the training can be beneficial, employees do not retain the information from outside vendors well because of lack of visuals or lack of instructor knowledge. In addition, resources are not being utilized when needed. One of those resources consists of the human resources function not being able to follow-up in an adequate amount of timing with other managers or employees in regard to training and resource information. In certain departments training programs are limited for employees by managers simply because are not required to attend even though it could be beneficial to understanding the "big picture" of their organization. Moreover, training is being performed on tasks that are considered obsolete. Employees find out information that is pertinent to their job by accidental discoveries that were never mentioned or trained on prior. Leaders are comfortable with the status quo and are challenged to stand up and make decisions for their department which affects the overall dynamic in behavior and communication with their respective employees.

Theories

Theories explain facts that have been tested where predictions were made about natural phenomena (Abend, 2008). They explain existing knowledge within the limits of critical bounding assumptions (Abend, 2008). The theoretical framework supports theories within the research. It introduces and describes the theory and why the research problem exists (Abend, 2008). The theories in this research are path-goal theory, transactional theory, and transformational theory.

Path-Goal Theory. Path-Goal Theory relates to the findings because it provides organization in understanding for needed effective training from leaders in order to strengthen leadership that provides skills and knowledge to employees which is meant to motivate them (Northouse, 2016). Leaders have to plan on setting goals in order to manage their time effectively so they can train employees. Path-Goal theory assumes the leaders have the responsibility to facilitate employee success.

Transactional Leadership Theory. Transactional leadership theory relates to the findings because it impacts the motivation of employees and their performance. Transactional leaders tend to decrease their employee engagement especially when it pertains to training. They are comfortable maintaining the status quo which hinders performance (Rodrigues & Ferreira, 2015). Time is not adequately dispersed with leaders that are transactional. Transactional leaders lack prioritizing training when needed (Rodrigues & Ferreira, 2015).

Transformational Leadership Theory. Transformational leadership theory relates to the findings because there are leaders in this government organization that have the ability to connect with their employees in an effort to motivate them toward achieving goals (Peng, Liao, & Sun, 2020). It is evident that there are events that bring the organization together as a whole and boost morale of managers, supervisors, and employees. The organizational culture fosters connection, independence, and self-ownership.

Actors

Actors influence the development of the research. They are key people that are vital to the research problem. The actors in this research are leaders, employees, and organizations.

Leaders. Leaders relate to the findings because they are managers and supervisors. The managers and supervisors set the tone of their department and ensure that tasks that need to be done are getting completed. They are the decision makers and delegate tasks to employees as well as have the responsibility to train them adequately. Leaders are held accountable for effectively training employees to the best of their abilities (Kirchner & Akdere, 2017).

Employees. Employees relate to the findings because they are the organization's personnel that are directly affected by training whether it is effective or ineffective. Either way it has a huge bearing on employee performance within the organization.

Organizations. Organizations relate to the findings of this research because this research was conducted in a local government organization. The government sector provided a broad scope of different departments training to employees from diverse leaders.

Constructs

A construct assists in explaining how and why certain phenomena behave the way they do. It provides a common language and shared meaning that help explain things clearly and precisely. The constructs of this research are training, organizational performance, and employee knowledge and skills.

Training. Training relates to the findings because it is the main topic of what the researcher is searching for understanding within a local government organization. It is also a theme that was indicated in this research. The kind of training can vary depending on the culture, resources, engagement, and challenges from a leader to an employee. Whether it is effective or ineffective it affects productivity and organizational performance. In addition, training affects employee turnover in which this organization has reported a high propensity of (Asfaw et al., 2015).

Organizational Performance. Organizational performance relates to the findings of this study because it identifies performance differences in employees that are effectively trained and employees that are ineffectively trained (March & Sutton, 1997).

Employee Knowledge and Skills. Employee knowledge and skills relates to the findings of this study because it contributes to how successful the organization is. Leaders that invest in their employees by training them effectively provide opportunities for growth and boost performance (Berglund & Andersson, 2012).

The Relationship of Anticipated Themes

The themes anticipated in the research are training contents, training environments, facilities and materials, training schedule, and presentation style. The first theme that was anticipated was training content. Training contents relate to the findings in this research because the leaders training process can have a huge impact on how the employee takes in leader training sessions. This includes instructor-led sessions, computer-based training, web-based training, and self-directed, interactive, or multimedia-inspired lessons. The material that was distributed within the organization to employees should be utilized. It is important to utilize all the material that is offered because it could sharpen the knowledge and skills of employees in addition to allowing the employee to better understand their position and promote growth.

The anticipated theme of training environment relates to the findings because it detracts from employee learning experience. For instance, when the researcher performed the interview for this organization, the participants felt comfortable because of the environment created. They were in a conference room, so they felt a sense of freedom to speak freely about their experiences. Training facilities is another theme that is anticipated. A selected facility meant for training provides a flexible environment for advanced learning. It was shown that employees adapt better to new situations; feel safe, and comfortable. The fourth theme of anticipation was training schedules. Training schedules in the organization are well scheduled for max training and training that is mandatory within the government for specific positions held. However, when it came to departmental training, leaders fell short. Scheduled training sessions within respective departments should be treated as much as a priority among leaders. According to Silverman (2015), training schedules help find effective solutions to related contingencies that may arise during the training process.

The last theme anticipated was presentation style because it has an effect on employee motivation. As stated by most participants within this research, they felt that training sessions that did not have visuals, guides, or instructors that engaged with the audience were deemed ineffective because they did not pay attention to what was being instructed. The presentation style helps employees learn as well as remember what they are being trained on. The instructor should think of training as a marketing tactic where they take inventory of their audience and try to appeal to their interests.

Relationship of the Literature

The findings that relate to the literature indicate that training practices that are ineffective have an impact on organizational performance from employees. Similarities in related studies suggest that training is potentially ineffective when it is not interactive with the audience. According to NG (2017), training that is effective from leaders to employees is shown to increase retention and enhance knowledge and skills. This is indicative of the problem facing this government organization. This government organization suffers from a high turnover rate due to training deficiencies according to the data analyzed. In addition, the author stated that training that is not interactive or engaging to employees is disengaging causing unmotivated learners. Even though 78.26% of participants experienced effective engagement with leaders, still 21.74% of participants were dissatisfied with engagement in their specific department. This signifies that those specific departments should be looked at and revamped to address the reasons for concern. According to Petkova (2011), "Optimizing Training Effectiveness: The Role of Regulatory Fit" favorable training outcomes from leaders match the employee's motivational orientation.

In related studies, organizations having adequate resources for their employees should be required and automatic (Nagar, 2009). The difference between this author's study and the current organization being researched is the lack of effective turnover or succession. Due to the organization's high turnover rate, their appropriate succession is being overlooked. It is documented that personnel in human resources are new (less than 5 months) and have been the only individual in that position. Just recently, there has been a job posting for an additional HR position. Moreover, data indicates that most departments within the organization rely on resource information for their specific job through Google. With updated guidance that is published generally yearly, there should be accountability for each department to store these guidance or regulations in a tangible binder for convenience and just in case technology is not available. Leaders and employees cannot just abandon their job because technology is not working. Being able to have "Post-Post" operations through training is imperative for each department to adopt. Al-Ajlouni, Athamneh, and Jaradat (2010) stressed that when evaluating training practices, there is a need to compare the output with other similar training programs. This comparison assists in identifying problems that lie within the leader and their department's specific training program.

According to Eidt (1992), individual's learning at a different pace and different ways of learning. This study suggested that training can impede time management because learning tasks as you go maximizes valuable time and production activities. The difference between the author's study and this current study is that participants disagree with finding things out as they go in their job or when it comes to completing a task. According to the researcher, participants feel that including training in leader time management makes it an important task in addition to fostering positive engagement. This allows for the leader and employee to close learning gaps and promote morale boosting. The researcher believes that teamwork instead of individual training is ineffective and counterproductive.

During the literature review, it was found that 94% of participants implied that training from leaders was ineffective. The training programs did not meet their expectations and needs. These findings were supported by Research Question 1 during the researcher's interview process. Similarly, Brimstin and Hester (2015) emphasized that the needs of the employees have to be considered when evaluating and conducting training programs. In addition, McNamara (2016) agreed leaders should evaluate training practices often to benefit not just the employees, but the performance needs and goals of the organization which in turn promotes job satisfaction and morale among employees. The author also notes that the reason why organizations conduct training programs is to prepare employees for upcoming changes, so they are able to adjust.

Application of Professional Practice

This study adds to the existing body of knowledge to develop strategies and provides knowledge on how the findings are relevant to exploring the impact of training, which may contribute to the effectiveness of organizational performance. Employee engagement is a key feature in high performance workplaces. It includes collaborative decision making, has a positive relationship with work attitudes and the engagement of employees (Brown et al., 2011). The results revealed that 82.60% of respondents had a positive attitude about their organizational culture because they believe that it is a great place to work despite training challenges. Most participants stated more engagement and effective training with leaders could improve organizational performance. When employees are not satisfied with their role in the organization, turnover rates increase (Nyberg, 2010). The lack of strategies that decrease barriers, improve incentives, and improve workplace relationships between management and employees might have an immense impact on organizations. It is important for leaders to understand how to develop strategies for positive organizational performance.

Improving General Leadership Practice

Effective training should be at the top of the agenda for organizations. Ineffective training in organizations was seen as an instrument for effective improvement and accountability for standards of learning. Organizational leaders are directly responsible for quality improvement as part of training through which organizations are accountable for improving the quality within the organization and maintaining high standards by creating an environment in which excellence in training will continuously develop. Quality has been defined as 'the degree to which training for individuals and groups increase the likelihood of desired outcomes and are consistent with current professional knowledge and includes the fundamental principles of effectiveness and employee experience; but improvement, which implies change for the better, should be more than this. For improvement to occur, leaders have to know how they are currently performing, understand what constitutes an improvement and have the skills to bring about change. Improvements in organizations require effective leadership, a culture supporting innovation, and the assimilation of technical skills and structures for coordinating and monitoring change. Culture is a shared set of values, ideas, concepts, and rules of behavior that allow a group to function and perpetuate itself. Cultural resistance is thought to arise from a lack of vision, poor organization, teamwork or attitudes and deficient learning. Leadership, culture and training are seen as essential elements of quality or effectiveness.

Organizational leaders should provide the initial framework for accountability and effectiveness, but knowledge and understanding about the importance of leading improvement, the culture of quality and usefulness of improvement methods. Uncertainty persists about whether training has demonstrated its anticipated benefits despite more positive recent appraisals. Previous research on leadership improvement has focused on structural change, process and outcomes and less on the development of effective leadership, culture for innovation or the use of improvement methods. Therefore, there is a need to understand the leadership behaviors of those tasked with change in general practice, to explore how this relates to the culture of organizations and to ascertain whether it has led to adoption of quality leadership improvement techniques that are likely to promote positive change. Moreover, although there has been over a decade of development of quality improvement a technique appropriate for general practice, there is limited evidence of the extent of their adoption. This study aims to understand the impact of training on organizational performance in government organizations.

Training is vital in the awareness across general leadership practice. Effective training should include everybody, including the managers and supervisors. Leader responsibilities should be clear. Whether it is intuitive actions based on experience and expertise in specific tasks or whether it is a result of organizational policies and procedures, effective leadership is key to any successful business. Training and building awareness can lead to a risk management culture that will drive business success. Honesty and integrity are the fundamental cornerstones of good leadership. Effective leaders are trustworthy and always have the best interests of the employees and the organization in mind. They hold themselves accountable for their actions and decisions and encourage their employees to do the same. Transparency is also important, even when there is negative information to share. Strong leaders find reasons to get the organization together and celebrate success, retirements, birthdays, and business success. Training effectively decreases turnover, saves costs through more efficient leadership practices, and workflow efficiencies. It creates a feeling of collaborative working and team support within an organization. Leaders that accept responsibilities for failures, even when they may have not been directly responsible, and give credit to others for their successes are effective leaders. It's important to foster trust and collaboration, thereby making it possible for others to perform at their best. Successful leaders put employees in leadership positions whether it is a new project, an ongoing program or an idea. They create ways for their employees to lead. In order to build the right team, they have to let them take be in decision making positions and be supportive and nurtured by picking them up when they fall short. Encouraging continuous improvement and learning from mistakes allow employees to feel a sense of empowerment. Effective leaders make tough decisions and are able to recognize when they need the expertise or knowledge of others.

The findings in this study show that 83.61% of participants feel that more engaged in-person training methods, less outside training vendors, and tangible resources can improve leadership practice. Most of the training is conducted on an individual's own time online where they can click through as many times to get the correct answer therefore making the information in the online training forgettable and wasteful. In addition, training that is required is desired to be a group effort that is engaging amongst the department. Participants noted that they would appreciate not being limited to training that is not required, but an employee shows interest in attending. Moreover, based on participant statements, changes in training methods by leaders are not discussed.

Training methods of what is effective and what is ineffective for the organization and department should be discussed and revamped often. Training is constant and should not be relied on as status quo for all. These changes would prove significant in improving leadership practices for this study.

Potential Implementation Strategies

The suggestions for training reflect the significance of Section 1 and conclusions presented in Section 2. The qualitative case study could close the gaps in related literature by providing additional perspectives into the strategic and operational decisions within organizations. The results of the study support the effects of training that are expounded on the understanding of behaviors that effectively influence organizational performance and therefore retain an effective organization. Individuals associated with strategic advantages use different forms of motivation to reduce ambiguities that constrain performance (Lechner, 2012). When individuals are not familiar with changes, retorts such as apprehension and stress become a challenge for organizational leaders. Leaders may receive positive insight and knowledge on reducing training barriers. Organizational leaders should understand that their responsibility to establish an environment that supports constant learning and enhancement of employees through effective training and other environmental elements. Findings show engagement may further highlight the importance of support for creating connections between leaders and employees that decrease stress and negative behaviors. Considering individuals from all backgrounds as valued members is a strategic element for any organization to survive (Dovidio, Saguy, & Gaertner, 2010).

In order to develop an effective organizational training strategy, it's important to follow a process that will help to identify the core requirements of the organization for training and qualifications. This process can be broken down into two phases. The first phase is creating a training plan that is effective, and the second phase is completing the strategic implementation. Developing an effective strategy for training forces the organization to look at their needs, goals and resources that are available. As for implementation, this phase requires constant monitoring, revisions, and verification. In order to create an effective training strategy, leaders have to establish an employee training plan. The training plan will effectively cover all of the theoretical needs within the organization with regard to employee development. In addition, it will also cover the training goals as well as their effects on employee competencies. Identifying critical employee training needs is the first step to developing an effective training plan. This usually involves analyzing new trends, marketing research, competitive strategy analysis and identifying what the organization needs when it comes to training. This can be accomplished by interviewing employees or creating a focus group. By interviewing employees or having a focus group, leaders will be able to identify and analyze areas within their specific department that need more training skill sets or additional qualifications.

This strategy will have the organization's employees from one point to another, along with the amount of time required to do it. By establishing a development gap, the organization will be able to set up a feasible framework for their training strategy, which makes the whole process easier to manage. Training goals are the training objectives of the training strategy. The organization's training action plan is when leaders implement the strategy. It ensures that the training strategy has access to the necessary funds as well as making preparations for acquiring the necessary resources, instructors, and venues in order to implement the training process. The second part of developing an organizational training strategy is implementation. It involves critical work that is necessary to make sure that the training strategy is put into practice. Implementing an organizational training strategy may also involve several phases and processes which include monitoring the training of employees, training evaluation, and making revisions to the training plan. Monitoring the training of employees conducted by leaders, and their goal is to make sure that the training strategy is achieving those goals that it is meant to achieve. It also seeks to measure the responsiveness of the trainees to their training. Training evaluation makes sure that the training strategy is achieving those goals that it is meant to achieve. In addition, it seeks to measure the responsiveness of the trainees to their training. Making revisions to the training plan happens when the organizational training strategy is not meeting all objectives, becomes obsolete, or redundant during implementation, then a few revisions to the training plan will be necessary to ensure the continued success of the training strategy.

Organizational development requires a good training strategy. This training strategy can take on different characteristics, but it has to service the developmental needs of the organization. This includes increased competency in critical areas, direct work experience for new employees or well-trained employees. In developing an organizational training strategy, it's important to pay attention to the "big picture" and to implement the necessary practices to meet long term strategic goals. The recommendations could support improved long-term sustainability strategies for leaders within an organization. The significance of exploring the effects of performance in the organization could potentially assist leaders in developing strategies to increase productivity, profitability and reduce barriers in the organization.

Summary of Application to Professional Practice

The purpose of this flexible single case study was to explore the impact of training on organizational performance within government organizations. During a structured interview, each participant will be asked the exact same question in the same order. This type of interview is an effective approach with participants that are selected through convenient sampling. Numbers 1 through 23 replaced participant names. The following were the research questions in the study: How do leaders fail to effectively train employees within an organization, how do employees inhibit their own training, and what type of training are effective and what types are ineffective? The researcher ensured the accuracy of data by repeating participant responses, asking for more clarification, and asking follow up questions. Participants were not comfortable with being recorded; however, detailed notes were approved, and they confirmed answers for clarification. The NVivo software allowed the researcher to organize large amounts of data and provide reliable data analysis (Hutchison et al., 2010).

Results show that 82.60% of respondents had a positive attitude about their organizational culture because they believe that it is a great place to work despite training challenges. The lack of strategies that decrease barriers, improve incentives, and improve workplace relationships between management and employees might have an immense impact on organizations.

Organizational leaders are directly responsible for quality improvement as part of a training through which organizations are accountable for continuously improving the quality within the organization and safeguarding high standards by creating an environment in which excellence in training will prosperously develop. For improvement to occur, leaders have to know how they are currently performing, understand what constitutes an improvement and have the skills to bring about change. Organizational leaders should provide the initial framework for accountability and effectiveness, but knowledge and understanding about the importance of leading improvement, the culture of quality and usefulness of improvement methods. There is therefore a need to understand the leadership behaviors of those tasked with change in general practice, to explore how this relates to the culture of organizations and to ascertain whether it has led to adoption of quality leadership improvement techniques that are likely to promote positive change. Training is vital in the awareness across general leadership practice. Building awareness can lead to a risk management culture that will drive business success. In addition, it decreases turnover, saves costs through more efficient leadership practices, and workflow efficiencies. Leaders are supposed to create ways for their employees to lead.

In order to develop an effective organizational training strategy, it's important to follow a process that will help to identify the core requirements of the organization for training and qualification. The first phase is creating a training plan that is effective, and the second phase is completing the strategic implementation. The second phase is implementation, which requires constant monitoring, revisions, and verifications. This strategy will have the organization's employees from one point to another, along with the amount of time required to do it. By establishing a development gap, the organization will be able to set up a feasible framework for their training strategy, which makes the whole process easier to manage. Making revisions to the training plan happens when the organizational training strategy is not meeting all objectives, becomes obsolete, or redundant in the course of implementation, then a few revisions to the training plan will be necessary to ensure the continued success of the training strategy. Having a good training strategy will increase competency in critical areas, direct work experience for new employees or well-trained employees.

Recommendations for Further Study

Leaders that develop organizational strategies could provide enhance employee abilities, motivation, and opportunities that increase performance. Effective leaders understand that their main objective is to enhance employee performance, but the lack of training strategies could have a negative impact on organizations. Samnani, Salamon, and Singh (2014) stated negative behaviors increase negative actions that increase barriers and high retention rates. The participants provided perceptiveness into the difficulties and challenges in the organization. The researcher recommends that organizational leaders assist with implementing strategies that improve communications between employees and their leaders. Organizational leaders could use the results of this study to improve organizational performance and decrease barriers and high retention rates. The majority of the participants interviewed had a positive attitude about organizational culture. Leaders should create a positive environment because it may increase employee productivity and decrease stress. Most participants noted that engagement barriers existed within the organization. Motivating employees could establish a better working environment and increase workflow. Leaders should contribute to the balance between work and non-work life to produce improved outcomes at work. Participants addressed issues about performance measures and training in the resources theme. Organizational leaders might consider providing more hands-on training that is energetic and engaging. Based on the study findings related to engagement, organizational leaders should consider improving communication which could improve work processes, employee engagement, and it may demonstrate leader concerns and respect for employee contributions. Based on findings in leadership challenges, leaders might consider making sure that they are trained effectively before training employees. In addition, they should seek ways to put employee training, encouragement, and acknowledgement as their top priorities. Providing incentives encourage motivation in the work environment and awards and recognition that reinforce employee engagement. Engaged employees are likely to be the organization's best source of innovation.

There are common variables such as lack of employee engagement with leaders and effective training resources that contribute to employee turnover rates and retention strategies. Findings depict that leaders who train employees effectively are more likely to maintain a valuable workforce over organizations that do not offer training. Training and other quality decisions affect the profitability of organizations. Yin (2011) noted that an interview acquires minimal additional information after 20 interviews. The researcher analyzed data from one specified organization located within the United States of America using a sample size of 23 participants.

Obtaining the experiences of participants from only one organization could have limited the application of results. Another limitation related to researching specific aspects of organizational performance rather than all components of performance in the organization. Due to the elements of organizational performance being a broad study, conducting further studies on career decisions and career paths could provide leaders with an abundance of resources to decrease barriers and increase performance. The recommendations in this research could assist the abilities of leaders in order to improve employee motivation, performance, leadership, engagement, and revenue. It is imperative for leaders to understand recruitment and retention strategies. Feldman and Tyler (2012) explored the relationship between employee experience in procedures related to adequate training and resources, and if employees' adherence to organizational based on training practices enacted by organizations leaders that are voluntarily or mandated. The findings from the study show employees responded positively to training that is aimed at individual development and are specific in career tasks in addition to engaging.

Reflections

The research process provides information on the problem from different perspectives. The data collection process allowed the researcher to communicate open ended questions based on training with participants. The participants did not have questions for concern in answering the questions and they seemed sincerely interested in the study topic. The researcher adhered to the interview protocol outlined in the research design by attempting to make participants comfortable and asked the interview questions in a conversational manner to develop a relaxed environment. This elicited genuine responses from the participants. The participants engaged in the interviews and appeared interested in the study topic. Coding and interpretation of data was more complicated than the researcher perceived, but using the software NVivo reinforced the suitability of themes and added validity to study findings. During the interviews, participants addressed concerns about engagement, training, and resources. All of the participants felt improving in these areas might decrease turnover and increase retention.

Personal & Professional Growth

This research topic provided insights and in-depth perspective to the researcher. The experience in researching the effects that training has on an organization's performance was beneficial for the researcher's professional and personal growth. What bought about this research topic was the researcher's experience as a Logistics Manager in the United States Air Force. In Logistics, there was a lot of training that was required, but far too often training was overlooked, leaders were not leading adequately, and basic communication was rare. A lot of the problems stem from the revolving door of leaders which caused constant organizational change. This is very common in the military. The researcher was very intrigued to discover what methods were effective for employees when it involved training from leaders. Having multicultural intelligence and knowing how to deal with others or how to motivate them to perform their work better was imperative to the study. Personally, as a former Non-Commissioned Officer, the researcher was considered to be a "micromanager" from several different leaders and employees. Not knowing that her way of managing was negative, this forced the researcher to reevaluate interaction with others and methods of training and communication. Conducting this research has been beneficial to the researcher's growth because by providing more perspective on how to effectively conduct qualitative research as well as achieve an educational desire that was never thought to be reached. The researcher believed in consistently challenging herself to be better and do better. Professionally, the researcher gained insight from leaders and employees in another organization on what training methods are effective, ineffective, how and when to provide adequate training, and engagement. In addition, this research helped with networking for career growth and future projects.

Biblical Perspective

This research topic examines how the business functions influence the Christian Worldview. Ethics is founded on the Christian scripture which is based on a moral standard and allows us to decide between right and wrong. In business, leaders have to decide what they have to do and what ethical principles to follow. A leader having a set of principles acknowledges that they know what is right and wrong and that their decision is reliable. Researchers and business leaders seek ethical standards and behaviors that are found in

Scripture. Decisiveness is a key to influential leadership. Individuals cannot follow a person that does not know where they are going or why they are going in the direction that they are going. Matthew 5:36, 37 states "And do not swear by your head, for you cannot make even one hair white or black. All you need to say is simply 'Yes' or 'No'; anything beyond this comes from the evil one" (NIV). The power to say yes or no quickly means that you know where you are going and what you are trying to accomplish. Make your words mean something. Develop and build trust relationships by conveying to others that they can count on you and your commitments. Many leaders lose their influence with others because they commit to aspirational yeses.

The Ten Commandments provide a foundation for laws in modern society which govern business practices. It includes truthfulness in business transactions such as training, engagement, and performance measures. Moreover, the Bible provides moral guidance in business. The parable of the rich fool and the parable of the talents teach about proper management of possessions and diligence in organizations. The primacy of love and service to others is consistent with the goals of corporate social responsibility (Calkins, 2000). It should be noted that simply citing a chapter and verse for the moral statement being made, or insisting that God has demanded it, is not sufficient to a make a Christian ethic (Rossouw, 1994). In addition, Christian ethics is not a set of isolated moral principles, but it is dependent upon prior Christian worldviews based on reality. This is expressed in the relationship between God and his savants. What is expressed in Scripture is not a set of principles or rules; instead, it is an understanding of reality. Christian ethics require the use of reason that is derived from Scripture narratives that guide human action and bring about certain consequences, primarily to pursue the idea of service to others (Calkins, 2000) and practicing good stewardship. According to Rossouw (1994), someone with a Christian understanding of the unconditional value of life, cannot be careless in the workplace about products and quality-standards that pose a threat to the lives of employees. Matthew 6:21 states that "Where your treasure is, there is where your heart will be also" (NIV). Investment is another term for treasure. Leaders are called to lead with passion or all of their heart. Therefore, a leader must make investments wisely. Leaders in businesses are called upon to make many investments. A leader must make use of the resources of the company to make the right investments in the business, people, and their organization. When businesses are invested wisely, the business will grow. Good investments set the direction and the path of a business to ensure its growth and development. When a business is neglected, it suffers. When effective training is neglected, employees suffer. Hosea 4:6 says, "My people are destroyed from lack of knowledge. Because you have rejected knowledge, I also reject you as my priests; because you have ignored the law of your God, I also will ignore your children" (NIV).

Approaching business ethics research from a Christian worldview requires individuals to re-think their assumptions and beliefs about religion and the nature of reality. It is a worldview that applies to all areas including social issues, history, politics, science, and anthropology (Pearcey, 2004). However, the assumption in modern society assumes that knowledge, truth, and morality are founded in science and reason, Christianity is based on the understanding that God was the creator of the universe, and that man, by use of his reason, could discover the mysteries of the world. Christian thinking is not opposed to science and scientific discoveries or to a rational understanding of the world as evidenced by research of scientists. Scripture has a lot to say about human nature and behavior that is consistent with what experienced. Given the challenge among business leaders to create a more ethical environment, ethics research from a Christian viewpoint could provide insights that promote morality within the organization.

Summary of Section 3

The findings preclude that the data analyzed supports presentation the conceptual framework and literature on the effects training and how it impacts organization performance. The researcher documented all data provided by participants on the interview questionnaire and structured guide. The interview process was over a 2-day period with 14 in-person interviews and 9 interviews conducted over the phone. The researcher ensured the data provided was accurate by validating the questions by asking the three follow-up questions which were the approved research questions. The three main research questions that impact this study are "How do leaders fail to effectively train employees within an organization", "How do employees inhibit their own training", and "What type of training are effective and what types are ineffective".

The triangulation method used in this study was data. This method examined patterns and contradictions for different participants at different times in order to show changes in participant experiences. The different groups in this study were (5) managers, (4) supervisors, and (14) employees. The researcher used the software NVivo to assist in organizing data in search of themes that were helpful in the process of analyzing data. The themes discovered were (a) culture, (b) engagement, (c) resources, (d) training practices, and (e) leadership challenges. The sub themes discussed in this study were performance management, tools and material, notice provided before training, job rotation, increase of productivity after training, and what constitutes as effective and ineffective training. The last sub theme is the actual basis of this research. Understanding what training practices are effective and what training practices are ineffective has a huge bearing on organizational performance.

The findings of this study in relate to the research framework because training that is effective cannot be accomplished if leader engagement is not present. It is imperative that leaders manage their time to include training their employees regularly. According to Northouse (2016), Path-goal theory assumes that leaders have the responsibility to facilitate the success of employees by setting goals. Leaders that were transactional tend to have less interaction or engagement with their employees which makes it easy for them to maintain the status quo instead of introducing new motivational tactics to enhance training. Leaders that were transformational connect to their employees and boost morale of all involved through motivation. The knowledge and skills of employees are honed after effective training which increases confidence and performance. The themes that were anticipated in this research were training contents, training environments, facilities and materials, training schedule, and presentation style. Training contents relate to the findings in this research because the leaders training process can have a huge impact on how the employee takes in leader training sessions. Training environment relates to the finding because it deters distracts from employee learning experiences. Training facilities provide a flexible environment for advanced learning. The final theme anticipated was presentation style because it helps employees learn as well as remember what they are being trained on. The findings in this literature indicate that there are similarities present to related literature on ineffective training. There is a high report on employee turnover, lack of adequate resources available, and a deficiency in departmental training practice as indicated in the transcribed data from participant experiences. The data supported the researcher's findings of 91.30% of participants, suggest that training from their leaders were not effective. Brimstin and Hester (2015) emphasized that the needs of the employees have to be considered when evaluating and conducting training programs. This promotes job satisfaction and boosts employee morale. When leaders are training employees, they should be able to gage and evaluate what practices are effective and ineffective for the employee benefit of development (McNamara, 2016).

Leaders that are effective understand that their main objective is to enhance employee performance. Lack of training strategies could have a negative impact on organizations. According to Samnani, Salamon, and Singh (2014), negative behaviors increase negative actions which increase barriers and high retention rates. Leaders should create a positive environment because it may increase employee productivity and decrease stress. Motivating employees could establish a better working environment and increase workflow. Organizational leaders might consider providing more hands-on training that is energetic and engaging. Based on the study findings related to engagement, organizational leaders should consider improving communication which could improve work processes, employee engagement, and it may demonstrate leader concerns and respect for employee contributions. In addition, findings depicted that leaders who train employees effectively are more likely to maintain a valuable workforce over organizations that do not offer training. Training and other quality decisions affect the profitability of organizations. The recommendations in this research could assist the abilities of leaders in order to improve employee motivation, performance, leadership, engagement, and revenue. It is imperative for leaders to understand recruitment and retention strategies. Participants engaged in the interviews and appeared interested in the study topic. Coding and interpretation of data was more complicated than the researcher perceived, but using the software NVivo reinforced the suitability of themes and added validity to study findings. During the interviews, participants addressed concerns about engagement, training, and resources. All the participants felt that improving these areas might decrease turnover and increase retention.

What bought about this research topic was the researcher's experience as a Logistics Manager in the United States Air Force. The researcher was very intrigued to discover what methods were effective for employees when it involved training from leaders. The researcher gained insight from leaders and employees in another organization on what training methods are effective, ineffective, how and when to provide adequate training, and engagement. In addition, this research helped with networking for career growth and future projects. The Bible provides moral guidance in business. The parable of the rich fool and the parable of the talents teach about proper management of possessions and diligence in organizations. The primacy of love and service to others is consistent with the goals of corporate social responsibility (Calkins, 2000). Christian ethics is not a set of isolated moral principles, but it is dependent upon prior Christian worldviews based on reality. This is expressed in the relationship between God and his savants. What is expressed in Scripture is not a set of principles or rules; instead, it is an understanding of reality. Christian ethics require the use of reason that is derived from Scripture narratives that guide human action and bring about certain consequences, primarily to pursue the idea of service to others (Calkins, 2000) and practicing good stewardship. Leaders in business are supposed to invest in people and their organization. When businesses are invested wisely, the business will grow and set good investments that are based on growth and development.

Chapter 10

Final Summary and Conclusions

This study examined the influence that training has on organizational performance. It further presents that organizational performance is significantly determined by training imparted to the employees from their leaders. An organization's performance relies on the commitment of employees, which in turn depends on the human resources policy on training. Effective training is important for organizational leaders because business trends demand more efficiency, accuracy, and effectiveness in less time and cost. This is achieved through the proper deployment of training practices from leaders to employees. By having an efficient training program in place to follow, employees will be interested to get more knowledge about their jobs which eventually assists them in getting promotions. It is imperative to reinforce and apply effective training as part of an organizational agenda in achieving organizational goals because it has a significant influence on an employee's commitment and performance.

Strategies are essential for organizational leaders to improve organizational performance. The researcher used convenience sampling during the interview process to explore the experiences of employees within this specified government organization. The findings revealed that most participants had a positive outlook on the organization's culture. In addition, participants addressed concerns about engagement, training, and resources. The findings may be beneficial to organizational awareness and the development of strategies to improve organizational performance. Employee turnover is a significant problem that negatively affects organizational performance (McKeown, 2010). It is recommended that leaders evaluate the needs of their employees and tailor strategies often to gain an optimal approach which will retain employees and decrease barriers.

References

Aarons, G. A., Ehrhart, M. G., Moullin, J. C., Torres, E. M., & Green, A. E. (2017). Testing the leadership and organizational change for implementation (LOCI) intervention in substance abuse treatment: A cluster randomized trial study protocol. *Implementation Science: IS, 12*(1), 29-29.

Abend, G. (2008). *The Meaning of Theory: Sociological Theory*. San Francisco, CA: Berrett-Koehler Publishers 2013.

Ahern, K. J. (1999). Ten tips for reflexive bracketing. *Qualitative Health Research.* (9) 407- 411.

Al-Ajlouni, M. M., Athamneh, M. H., Jaradat, A. A. (2010). Methods of evaluation: Training techniques international research. *Journal of Finance and Economics, 37*, 56-65.

Allen, M. R., Ericksen, J., & Collins, C. J. (2013). Human resource management, employee exchange relationships, and performance in small businesses. *Human Resource Management, 52*, 153-173.

Altrichter, H., Posch, P. & Somekh, B. (1996) *Teachers investigate their work: An introduction to the methods of action research*. London: Routledge.

Antonakis, J., Avolio, B. J., & Sivasubramaniam, N. (2003). Context and leadership: An examination of the nine-factor full range leadership theory using the Multifactor Leadership Questionnaire. *The Leadership Quarterly, 14*, 261-295

Armstrong, M. (2009). *Armstrong's Handbook of Human Resource Management Practice.* 11th Edition, Kogan Page Limited, London.

Asfaw, A., Argaw, M. and Bayissa, L. (2015). The Impact of Training and Development on Employee Performance and Effectiveness: A Case Study of District Five Administration Office, Bole Sub-City, Addis Ababa, Ethiopia. *Journal of Human Resource and Sustainability Studies, 3*, 188-202.

Ashworth, P. (1999). *Bracketing in Phenomenology.Qualitative.Studies in Education 12*(6): 707–721.

Beheshtifar, M., & Nazarian, R. (2013). Role of occupational stress in organizations. *Interdisciplinary Journal of Contemporary Research in Business, 4*, 648-657.

Berglund, L., & Andersson, P. (2012). Recognition of knowledge and skills at work: In whose interests? *Journal of Workplace Learning, 24*(2), 73-84.

Bickle, J. T. (2017). Developing remote training consultants as Leaders—Dialogic/Network application of Path-Goal leadership theory in leadership development. *Performance Improvement (International Society for Performance Improvement), 56*(9), 32-39

Birt, L., Scott, S., Cavers, D., Campbell, C., & Walter, F. (2016). Member Checking: A Tool to Enhance Trustworthiness or Merely a Nod to Validation? *Qualitative Health Research, 26*(13), 1802–1811.

Brannick, T., & Coghlan, D. (2016). In defense of being "Native": The case for insider academic research. *Organizational Research Methods, 10*(1), 59-74.

Breevaart, K., Bakker, A., Hetland, J., Demerouti, E., Olsen, O. K., & Espevik, R. (2014). Daily transactional and transformational leadership and daily employee engagement. *Journal of occupational and organizational psychology, 87*(1), 138-157

Brimstin, J., & Hester, A. (2015). *Training evaluation: Knowing what to measure.*

Brown, S., McHardy, J., McNabb, R., & Taylor, K. (2011). Workplace performance, worker commitment, and loyalty. *Journal of Economics & Management Strategy, 20*, 925-95.

Burke, P.J. (2003). *Relationships Among Multiple Identities in Advances in Identity Theory and Research*. New York: Kluwer Academic/Plenum. 195-214.

Burns, N & Grove, SK. 2001. *The practice of nursing research: conduct, critique and utilization*. 4th edition. Philadelphia: WB Saunders.

Cailler, J. G. (2014). Toward a better understanding of the relationship between transformational leadership, public service motivation, mission valence, and employee performance: A preliminary study. *Public Personnel Management, 43*, 218-239.

Cameron, K. S. (2012). *Positive leadership: Strategies for extraordinary performance*. Oakland, CA: Berrett-Koehler Publishers.

Caputi, P., Viney, L., Walker, B., Crittenden, N. (2011). *Personal Construct Methodology*. John Wiley & Sons, Ltd

Cho, Y. J., & Lewis, G. B. (2011). Turnover intention and turnover behavior: Implications for retaining federal employees. *Review of Public Personnel Administration, 32*(1), 4-23.

Claessens, B. J. C., van Eerde, W., Rutte, C. G., & Roe, R. A. (2007). A review of time management literature. *Personnel Review, 36*(2), 255-276.

Cianciolo, A.T. & Sternberg, R.J. (Eds). *The Nature of Leadership*. Sage Publications, Thousand Oaks, CA, pp. 101-24.

Cockerell, L. (2009). *Creating leadership magic. Leader to Leader*, Summer, 31-6.

Cohen, L., Manion, L., & Morrison, K. (2007). *Research Methods in Education*. 6th Ed. London: Routledge.

Cole, G.A. (2002). *Personnel and Human Resource Management*. 5th Edition, York Publishers, Continuum London.

Collier, W., Green, F., Kim, Y., & Peirson, J. (2011). Education, training and economic performance: Evidence from establishment survival data. *Journal of Labor Research, 32*, 336-361.

Conger, J. and Toegel, J. (2003). Action learning and multi-rater feedback as leadership development interventions: popular but poorly developed. *Journal of Change* Management, 3(4), 332-49

Creswell, John W. (2014). *Research design: Qualitative, quantitative and mixed methods approach* (4th ed.). Thousand Oaks, CA: Sage.

Creswell, J. W. (2009). *Research Design Qualitative, Quantitative, and Mixed Methods Approaches* (3rd ed.). Thousand Oaks, CA Sage Publications.

Creswell, J.W. & Miller, D. (2010). *Determining Validity in Qualitative Inquiry.*Theory into Practice.*39*(3) 124–30.

Creswell, J.W. and Plano Clark, V.L. (2011*) Designing and Conducting Mixed Methods Research*. 2nd Edition, Sage Publications, Los Angeles.

Creswell, J.W. & Poth, J. (2018). *Qualitative Inquiry & Research Design—Choosing among Five Approaches.*4th Edition, Sage Publications, London.

Denzin N.K, Lincoln Y.S. (2000). *Handbook of Qualitative Research*. London: Sage Publications.

Dezso, C. L., & Ross, D. (2012). Does female representation in top management improve firm performance? A panel data investigation. *Strategic Management Journal, 33,* 1072-1089.

Dovidio, J. F., Saguy, T., & Gaertner, S. L. (2010). Appreciating the role of the "individual mind" in diversity science: Commodity, harmony, and social change. *Psychological Inquiry, 21,* 108-114.

Dyer, L., & Reeves, T. (1995). Human resource strategies and firm performance: What do we know and where do we need to go? *International Journal of Human Resource Management*, *6*(3), 656– 670

Eidt, C. M., Jr. (1992). Applying Quality to R&D Means 'Learn-As-You-Go'. *Research Technology Management*, *35*(4), 24.

Einarsen, S., Aasland, M.S. and Skogstad, A. (2007). Destructive leadership behavior: a definition and conceptual model. *The Leadership Quarterly*. *18*(3), 207-216

EL Hajjar, S. T., & Alkhanaizi, M. S. (2018). Exploring the Factors That Affect Employee Training Effectiveness: A Case Study in Bahrain. *SAGE Open*.

Ellis, T. J., & Levy, Y. (2009). Towards a guide for novice researchers on research methodology: Review and proposed methods. *Issues in Informing Science and Information Technology*, *6*, 323-337.

Farhan, B. Y. (2018). Application of path-goal leadership theory and learning theory in A learning organization. *Journal of Applied Business Research*, *34*(1), 13-22

Feldman, Y., & Tyler, T. R. (2012). Mandated justice: The potential promise and possible 105 pitfalls of mandating procedural justice in the workplace. *Regulation & Governance*, *6*, 46-65.

Fernández-Esquinas, M., Pinto, H., Yruela, M. P., & Pereira, T. S. (2016). Tracing the flows of knowledge transfer: Latent dimensions and determinants of university–industry interactions in peripheral innovation systems. *Technological Forecasting & Social Change, 113*, 266-279.

Galletta, M., Portoghese, I., & Battistelli, A. (2011). Intrinsic motivation, job autonomy and turnover intention in the Italian healthcare: The mediating role of affective commitment. *Journal of Management Research, 3*, 1-19.

G. J. Rossouw (1994). Business Ethics in Developing Countries. *Business Ethics Quarterly 4* (1):43-51.

Gumusluoğlu, L., & Ilsev, A. (2009). Transformational leadership and organizational innovation: the roles of internal and external support for innovation. *Journal of Product Innovation Management, 26*(3), 264-277.

Golafshani, N (2003) *Understanding reliability and validity in qualitative research*. The Qualitative Report *8*(4): 597–606.

Griffin, R. W., & O'Leary-Kelly, A. M. (2004). *The Dark Side of Organizational Behavior*. New York: Wiley.

Hamill, C., & Sinclair, H. (2010). *Bracketing-practical considerations in Husser Lian phenomenological research*. Nurse Researcher, 17, 16-24.

Harvey, P., Stoner, J., Hochwarter, W. & Kacmar, C. (2007). Coping with abusive supervision: the neutralizing effects of ingratiation and positive affect on negative employee outcomes.*The Leadership Quarterly, 18*(3), 264-268

Hennink, M., Kaiser, B. (2019). *Saturation in Qualitative Research*. Sage Publications.Inc., Thousand Oaks

Heldenbrand, L., & Simms, M. S. (2012). Missing link: Integrated individual leadership development, employee engagement, and customer value-added improvement. *Performance Improvement, 51*(2), 28-25

Higgs, M. & Rowland, D. (2005). All changes great and small: exploring approaches to change and its leadership. *Journal of Change Management, 5*(2) 51-121.

Holbraad, M., Green, S., Corsín Jiménez, A., Das, V., Bird-David, N., Kohn, E., Hage, G., Bear, L., Knox, H., & Kapferer, B. (2018). What is analysis? Between theory, ethnography, and method. *Social Analysis, 62*(1), 1-30.

House, R. (1971). A Path Goal Theory of Leader Effectiveness. *Administrative Science Quarterly,16*(3), 321-339.

Hu, Z., & Qin, J. (2018). Generalizability of causal inference in observational studies under retrospective convenience sampling. Statistics in Medicine, *37*(19), 287-288.

Hughes, A. M., Zajac, S., Woods, A. L., & Salas, E. (2020). The role of work environment in training sustainment: A meta-analysis. *Human Factors, 62*(1), 166-183.

Hutchison, A., Johnston, L., & Breckon, J. (2010). Using QSR-NVivo to facilitate the development of a grounded theory project: an account of a worked example. *International Journal of Social Research Methodology, 13*, 283-302.

Jeelani, I., Albert, A., Azevedo, R., & Jaselskis, E. J. (2017). Development and testing of personalized hazard-recognition training intervention. *Journal of Construction Engineering and Management, 143*(5), 4016120.

Judge, T., Bono, J., Ilies, R. & Gerhardt, M.W. (2002). Personality and leadership: a qualitative and quantitative review. Journal of Applied Psychology, *87*, 765-80

Jung, D. I., Chow, C., & Wu, A. (2003). The role of transformational leadership in enhancing organizational innovation: Hypotheses and some preliminary findings. *The leadership quarterly, 14*(4), 525-544.

Kavitha, S. R., Geetha, S. R., & Arunachalam, V. (2011). An empirical study on employee retention strategies in a biscuit manufacturing company in India. *Interdisciplinary Journal of Contemporary Research in Business, 3*, 762-772.

Kellerman, B. (2004). Bad Leadership: What It Is, How It Happens, Why It Matters, Harvard *Business School Press, Boston, MA*

Kennedy, P. (2009). *How to combine multiple research options: Triangulation.* Washington, D.C.:World Bank

Kim, D., Fisher, D., & McCalman, D. (2009). Modernism, Christianity, and Business Ethics: A Worldview Perspective. *Journal of Business Ethics, 90*(1), 115–121.

Kirchner, M. & Akdere, M. (2017). Military leadership development strategies: implications for training in non-military organizations. *Industrial and Commercial Training, 49*(7), 357-364.

Kodwani, A. D., & Prashar, S. (2019). Exploring the influence of pre-training factors on training effectiveness-moderating role of trainees' reaction: A study in the public sector in india. *Human Resource Development International, 22*(3), 283-304.

Konecki, K. T. (2018). Classic grounded Theory — The latest version: Interpretation of classic grounded theory as a Meta-Theory for research. *Symbolic Interaction, 41*(4), 547-564.

Kozlowski, S. (2012). *The Oxford Handbook of Organizational Psychology*, Oxford University Press, New York.

Kroll, A., & Moynihan, D. P. (2015). Does training matter? Is there evidence from performance management reforms. *Public Administration Review, 75*(3), 411-420.

Kuhnert, K. W., & Lewis, P. (2017). Transactional and transformational leadership: A constructive/developmental analysis. *Academy of Management review, 12*(4), 648-657.

Lechner, C., & Floyd, S. W. (2012). Group influence activities and the performance of strategy. *Strategic Management Journal, 5*, 478-495.

Leedy, P. D., & Ormrod, J. E. (2019). *Practical research. Planning and design* (12th ed.). Boston, MA: Pearson

Legood, A., Lee, A., Schwarz, G., & Newman, A. (2018). From self-defeating to other defeating: Examining the effects of leader procrastination on follower work outcomes. *Journal of*

Occupational and Organizational Psychology, 91(2), 430-439.

Lindebaum, D., & Zundel, M. (2013). Not quite a revolution: Scrutinizing organizational neuroscience in leadership studies. *Human Relations, 66*(6), 857-877.

Lodico, M., Spaulding, D. T., & Voegtle, K. H. (2010). *Methods in educational research: From theory to practice.* San Francisco, CA: John Wiley & Sons.

Longenecker, C.O. (2010). Barriers to managerial learning: lessons for rapidly changing organizations. *Development and Learning in Organizations: An International Journal, 24*(5), 8-11.

Longenecker, C.O. (2010). Coaching for better results: key practices of high-performance leaders. *Industrial and Commercial Training, 42*(1), 32-40.

Louchakova-Schwartz, O. (2018). Phenomenology and theological research. *Open Theology, 4*(1), 640-644.

Low, K. C., & Ang, S. L. (2012). Confucian leadership and corporate social responsibility (CSR): The way forward. *Journal of Business Research, 2*(1), 85- 101.

Macan, T.H. (1996). Time-management training: effects on time behaviors, attitudes, and job performance. *The Journal of Psychology,130*(1), 229-36.

March, J. G., & Sutton, R. I. (1997). Organizational performance as a dependent variable. *Organization Science (Providence, R.I.), 8*(6), 698-706.

Marrelli, A. F. (2011). Employee engagement and performance management in the federal sector. *Performance Improvement, 50*(5), 5-13

Marshall, C., & Rossman, G. B. (2011). *Designing qualitative research* (5th ed.). Thousand Oaks, CA: Sage Publications, Inc.

Maxwell, J. A. (1996). *Qualitative research: An interactive approach*. Thousand Oaks, CA: Sage.

McNamara, C. (2016). Employee training and development: Reasons and benefits.

Melé, D., & Fontrodona, J. (2016;2017;). Christian ethics and spirituality in leading business organizations: Editorial introduction. *Journal of Business Ethics, 145*(4), 671-679.

Mendes, F., & Stander, M. W. (2011). Positive organization: The role of leader behavior in work engagement and retention. *SA Journal of Industrial Psychology, 37*(1), 1-13.

Mertens, D. M. (2008). Mixed Methods and the Politics of Human Research. In Clark, V. P., & Creswell,

J.W (eds). *The Mixed Methods Reader*. California: Sage.

Mollick, E. (2012). People and process, suits and innovators: the role of individuals in firm performance. *Strategic Management Journal, 33,* 1001-1015.

Nagar, V. (2009). Measuring training effectiveness. *The Indian Journal of Commerce, 62*(4), 86-90.

Natow, R. S. (2020). The use of triangulation in qualitative studies employing elite interviews. *Qualitative Research*: QR, *20*(2), 160-173.

Neuman, W. L. (2011). *Social research methods: Qualitative and quantitative approaches* (7th ed.). Boston, MA: Pearson.

NG, C. K. (2017). A complete project environment simulation to improve six sigma training class engagement. *International Journal of Quality Innovation, 3*(1), 1-15.

Northouse, P.G. (2016). *Leadership: Theory and practice (7th ed.).* Thousand Oaks, CA: Sage Publishers, Inc.

Oppenheim, A. (1992). *Questionnaire Design, Interviewing and Attitude Measurement.* Pinter, London. Publishers Ltd

Orey, M. (2014). Create an effective learning environment. *Sage*

Paauwe, J. (2004). *HRM and performance: Achieving long-term viability*. Oxford: Oxford University Press.

Padilla, A., Hogan, R. & Kaiser, R.B. (2007). The toxic triangle: destructive leaders, susceptible followers, and conducive environments. *The Leadership Quarterly, 18*(3), 176-194.

Pearcey, N.(2004). *Total Truth: Liberating Christianity from Its Cultural Captivity*. Wheaton, IL: Crossway.p.479.

Peeters, M.A.G. and Rutte, C.G. (2005). Time management behavior as a moderator for the job-demand-control interaction. *Journal of Occupational Health Psychology, Vol. 10, pp. 64-75.*

Peng, S., Liao, Y., & Sun, R. (2020). The Influence of Transformational Leadership on Employees' Affective Organizational Commitment in Public and Nonprofit Organizations: A Moderated Mediation Model. *Public Personnel Management. 49*(1):29-56.

Petkova, Z. (2011). Optimizing training effectiveness: The role of regulatory fit. *The University of Akron, OH*.

Popper, M. (2001). *The Relationship between Vision Strength, Leadership Style & Context*. The Leadership Quarterly, 12, 53-73.

Pozzebon, M. (2017). Beyond positivistic qualitative research. *Revista De administração De emprêsas, 57*(4), 415.

Purcell, Kinnie, and Hutchinson (2003). *Understanding the People and Performance Link: Unlocking the Black-Box.* Research Report, CIPD, London.

Ramachandran, R. (2010). Effectiveness of training programs of NLC—An Analysis. *Kegees Journal of Social Science, 2(1), 119-129*

Rauch, A., & Hatak, I. (2016). A meta-analysis of different HR-enhancing practices and performance of small and medium sized firms. *Journal of Business Venturing, 31*(5), 485– 504.

Robinson, J. L. (2016). Connecting leadership and learning: Do versatile learners make connective leaders? *Higher Learning Research Communications, 6*(1), 35. doi:10.18870/hlrc. v6i1.293.

Robson, C. (2002) *Real world research: A resource for social scientists and practitioner-researchers*, vol. 2, Blackwell Oxford.

Rodrigues, A. d. O., & Ferreira, M. C. (2015). The impact of transactional and transformational leadership style on organizational behaviors. *Psico Usf, 20*(3), 493-504.

Ross, R. (2012). Managing perfectionism in the workplace. *Employment Relations Today (Wiley), 39,* 1-6.

Ruark, B. E. (2010). Questioning minds on the lookout for potential workplace research and improvement markers: Practice-based research. *Performance Improvement, 10,* 15-19.

Sarfraz, H. (2017). Differentiated time management skills between leadership styles: Simplified with a cross-cultural approach. *Development and Learning in Organizations, 31*(6), 14-18.

Samnani, A., Salamon, S., & Singh, P. (2014). Negative affect and counterproductive workplace behavior: The moderating role of moral disengagement and gender. *Journal of Business Ethics, 119,* 235-244.

Sanjeevkumar, V., Yanan, H. (2011). Factors and its impact on training effectiveness in Kedah state development corporation, a study on training Kedah, Malaysia. *International Journal of Human Resource Studies, 1(2).*

Santhanam, N., T.J, K., Dyaram, L., & Ziegler, H. (2017). Impact of human resource management practices on employee turnover intentions. *Journal of Indian Business Research, 9*(3), 212-228.

Schaubroeck, J., Walumbwa, F.O., Ganster, D.C., Kepes, S., (2007). Destructive leader traits and the neutralizing influence of an "enriched" job. *The Leadership Quarterly* 18, 236-251.

Silverman, J. (2015). The key to an effective employee training plan schedule.

Smith, D. (2009). Making management count: A case for theory- and evidence-based public management. *Journal of Policy Analysis and Management, 28*(3), 497-505.

Sparks, J. R., & Pan, Y. (2010). Ethical judgments in business ethics research: Definition, and research agenda. *Journal of Business Ethics, 91*(3), 405-418.

Stone-Romero, E. F. (2002). *The relative validity and usefulness of various empirical research designs.* (77-98).

Susomrith, P., Coetzer, A., & Ampofo, E. (2019). Training and development in small professional services firms. European Journal of Training and Development, *43*(5/6), 517-535.

Su, N. (2018). Positivist qualitative methods. In Cassell, C., Cunliffe, A. L., & Grandy, G. *The sage handbook of qualitative business and management research methods*, City Road, London: SAGE Publications Ltd. 55, 17-31.

Swart, J., Mann, C., Brown, S. & Price, A. (2005). *Human*

Resource Development:

    Strategy and Tactics. Oxford. Elsevier Butterworth-Heinemann Publications.

Tharenou, P., Saks, A. M., & Moore, C. (2007). A review and critique of research on training

    and organizational-level outcomes. *Human Resource Management Review, 17*(3), 251– 273.

Taylor, J. (2014). Organizational culture and the paradox of performance management. *Public*

    Performance & Management Review, 38, 7-22.

The Holy Bible. (2020) English Standard Version. https://biblegateway.com (Original work

    published in 2001).

Urquhart C. (2013). *Grounded Theory for Qualitative Research: A Practical Guide.* Thousand Oaks: Sage.

Van De Mieroop, D., & Vrolix, E. (2014). A discourse analytical perspective on the professionalization of the performance appraisal interview. *Journal of Business Communication, 51,* 159-182.

Watkins, D. C. (2017). Rapid and Rigorous Qualitative Data Analysis. *International Journal of Qualitative Methods, 16*(1).

Webster, L., & Mertowa, P. (2007). Using narrative inquiry as a research method: an introduction to using critical event narrative analysis research on learning and teaching. *Oxon: Routledge.*

Wireman, T. (2010). *Training Programs for Organizations*. New York: Industrial Press Inc.

Wratcher, M.A. and Jones, R.O. (1988). A time management workshop for adult learners. *Journal of College Student Personnel,27* (1), 566-567.

Wright, P. & Geroy, D. G. 2001. Changing the mindset: the training myth and the need for word-class performance. *International Journal of Human Resource Management* 12,4, 586–600.

Yin, R.K. (2009). Case study research: design and methods. *Thousand Oaks, Calif. Sage Publications.*

Yiwen, Z., Lepine, J. A., Buckman, B. R., & Feng, W. (2014). It's not fair...or is it? The role of justice and leadership in explaining work stressor–job performance relationships. *Academy of Management Journal, 57,* 675-697.

Zaccaro, S.J., Kemp, C. & Bader, P. (2004). Leader traits and attributes. *Journal of Training and Development, 41*(6), 24-39.

Zhang, Q., MacKenzie, N. G., Jones-Evans, D., & Huggins, R. (2016). Leveraging knowledge as a competitive asset? The intensity, performance and structure of universities' entrepreneurial knowledge exchange activities at a regional level. Small Business Economics, 47(3), 657-675.

Appendix: Interview Questionnaire

Participant Number:

Circle One: Manager Supervisor   Employee

☐   By checking this box, I acknowledge that the information filed in this document is accurate and true. I also agree with the use of this information for research purposes.

Section 1: Demographic Information

What is your age? 20-24 ☐   25-29 ☐   30-34 ☐   35-39 ☐   40-44 ☐

What is your gender? ☐ Male ☐ Female ☐ Other: _____

What is your race? ☐ White ☐ Hispanic or Latino ☐ Black or African American ☐ Native American or American Indian ☐ Asian/Pacific Island Other:_____

How long have you been working for the organization?

☐ 0-4 ☐ 5-9 ☐ 10-14 ☐ 15-19 ☐ 20-24 ☐ 25-29 ☐ 30-34 ☐
☐ 35-39 ☐ 40-44

Section 2: Interview Questions

1. Tell me how often the organization conducts training for the employees?
2. Describe how much notice is given before training is conducted?
3. How do employees conduct their own training?
4. What are the training materials used for training?
5. Describe how productivity is increased after training?
6. What are the performance standards measured by?
7. Do employees that are not skilled in specific departments work in those departments if needed?
8. How often is job rotation?
9. Is there anything that you would like to add?

Afterword

As I close the final pages of this work, I find myself reflecting not only on the journey of writing this book, but on the greater journey of leadership — a path that has been both humbling and transformative.

This book was birthed from a place of purpose, tested through seasons of pressure, and carried forward by faith. It is more than research and theory; it is the result of lived experiences, spiritual insight, and an unwavering desire to help others lead with clarity, conviction, and compassion.

To every reader who found themselves somewhere within these pages — thank you. Whether you are a seasoned leader, an emerging voice, or someone still waiting to step into your calling, I see you. My prayer is that this book reignited your purpose and reminded you that your leadership is needed, valued, and sacred.

I wrote this book not to add to the noise, but to amplify what matters: people, purpose, and transformation. As leaders, we carry a responsibility to train others well, to steward influence wisely, and to lead in a way that

leaves others better than we found them. This is not the end — it's just the beginning.
So go forward. Lead boldly. Train purposefully. Live fully.

With gratitude and grace,
Dr. Sukoya T. Johnson, DSL
Founder, Ten'e Publishing House

"Commit your works to the Lord, and your plans will succeed." — Proverbs 16:3 (NASB)

Acknowledgements

Writing this book has been one of the most transformative experiences of my life, and I'm deeply grateful to everyone who stood beside me along the way.

To my family — thank you for your prayers, your encouragement, and for holding space for me when I needed to grow through the process.

To my mentors and spiritual leaders — thank you for pouring wisdom into me and reminding me to always lead from a place of purpose and faith.

To my brothers and sisters in the military — your discipline and example continue to inspire me.

And to every reader holding this book: thank you. My deepest hope is that this work equips and empowers you to lead with excellence, grace, and intention.

About the Author

Dr. Sukoya T. Johnson is a Retired United States Air Force Veteran, accomplished scholar, and passionate educator. She holds a Doctorate in Strategic Leadership in Business from Liberty University, an MBA from Rutgers University, a Bachelor of Science degree in Organizational Dynamics from Wilmington University, an Associate of Applied Science degree in Logistics from The Community College of the Air Force, and a Certificate in Elementary Education from the University of Phoenix. She is also a certified educator dedicated to shaping minds and building leaders.

With over two decades of combined military, educational, and leadership experience, Dr. Johnson brings a powerful blend of discipline, insight, and compassion to the world of organizational development. Her work centers on helping leaders unlock their potential, transform team dynamics, and create purpose-driven cultures that last.

Leading with Purpose: The Transformative Power of Training on Organizational Performance is a culmination of her research, her mission, and her belief that with the right training, people and organizations can truly thrive.